# RESISTANCE BANDS FOR SENIORS

## *50, 60 and Beyond*

***Home Strength Training, Improve Flexibility and Regain Muscle safely using inexpensive bands. Fully illustrated, 32 workouts + 80 videos***

DAVID O'CONNOR

# FREE BONUS FITNESS MATERIAL TO HELP YOU ACHIEVE YOUR GOAL

To ensure you gain as much value as possible from Resistance Bands For Seniors, I've put together some additional free bonus materials to help you achieve your goals, including:

- **32 Workout Plans** provided as printable PDF documents (8 each for Beginners, Intermediate, Seated and Advanced).
- **4 fitness Word Puzzles**. As a bit of fun to help maintain brain fitness too.
- **Direct access to the exercise videos** from our members area (without scanning QR Codes)

- **Members Only Access** to videos showing the exercises contained in each of the 32 workout plans (not available from within the book via QR codes)
- **Monthly Newsletter** on topics to help you succeed on your fitness journey.

**GET YOUR FREE BONUS MATERIAL**

# TABLE OF CONTENTS

**Foreword** . . . . . . . . . . . . . . . . . . . . . . . . . . . . . 13
**Introduction** . . . . . . . . . . . . . . . . . . . . . . . . . . . 15
What if There Were a Way for You to Become Stronger? . . . . . . . . . . . . . . . . . . . . . . 15
Resistance Band Training . . . . . . . . . . . . . . . . . . . . . 16
In this book, you'll learn: . . . . . . . . . . . . . . . . . . . . . 17
Meet the Author . . . . . . . . . . . . . . . . . . . . . . . . . . 22

**Chapter 1:** Resistance Band Basic Workouts . . . . . . 27
Safely Benefitting and Building Every Part of Your Body . . . . . . . . . . . . . . . . . . . . . 27
The Basics . . . . . . . . . . . . . . . . . . . . . . . . . . . . . . 29
How the Bands Are Used . . . . . . . . . . . . . . . . . . . . . 30
Benefits of Resistance Bands . . . . . . . . . . . . . . . . 33
Best for Seniors . . . . . . . . . . . . . . . . . . . . . . . . . . . 36
Get Checked Out . . . . . . . . . . . . . . . . . . . . . . . . . . 37
What About Pain? . . . . . . . . . . . . . . . . . . . . . . . . . 38

**Chapter 2:** Benefits of Resistance Band Workouts . . 40

Look Better, Feel Better, Be Better . . . . . . . . . . . . 40
How Resistance Bands Protect Your Skeleton . . . 41
About Osteoporosis . . . . . . . . . . . . . . . . . . . . . . . . . 42
Why Does It Happen? . . . . . . . . . . . . . . . . . . . . . . . 42
Research Confirms the Efficacy of Resistance Bands . . . . . . . . . . . . . . . . . . . . . . . . . 44
Additional Advantages to Resistance Bands . . . . 47
Many Weight Lifters Give Up . . . . . . . . . . . . . . . . . 48
Why Resistance Bands Are So Effective . . . . . . . . 49
Physical Changes You Can Expect . . . . . . . . . . . . 51
Consistency Is Key to Results . . . . . . . . . . . . . . . 52

**Chapter 3:** An Introduction to Resistance Bands . . . 55

Knowing What to Buy and How to Use . . . . . . . . . 55
Low Cost and Compact . . . . . . . . . . . . . . . . . . . . . 56
Bands, Tubes, or Both? Different Types of Resistance Bands . . . . . . . . . . . . . . . . . . . . . . . . . 57
Where to Purchase . . . . . . . . . . . . . . . . . . . . . . . . . 65
Using Your Bands: Some Safety Tips . . . . . . . . . . 66

**Chapter 4:** Beginner Resistance Band Exercises . . . 69

Enthusiasm Tempered by Caution . . . . . . . . . . . . 69
Preparation . . . . . . . . . . . . . . . . . . . . . . . . . . . . . . 70
Warm Up and Breathing . . . . . . . . . . . . . . . . . . . . 72
Reps and Sets . . . . . . . . . . . . . . . . . . . . . . . . . . . . 74

**Beginner Resistance Band Exercises . . . . . . . . . . . 76**
Chest Pull Apart #1 . . . . . . . . . . . . . . . . . . . . 78
Lat Pulldown #2 . . . . . . . . . . . . . . . . . . . . . . 80
Seated Row #3 . . . . . . . . . . . . . . . . . . . . . . . 82
Pallof Press #4 . . . . . . . . . . . . . . . . . . . . . . 86
Band Side Step #5 . . . . . . . . . . . . . . . . . . . . 88
Clamshell #6 . . . . . . . . . . . . . . . . . . . . . . . 90
Side Leg Lift #7 . . . . . . . . . . . . . . . . . . . . . 92
Chest Press #8 . . . . . . . . . . . . . . . . . . . . . . 94

**Chapter 5:** Intermediate Resistance Band Exercises . . 98

Moving up and Getting Stronger . . . . . . . . . . . . . 98

**Lower Body Intermediates . . . . . . . . . . . . . . . . . 100**
Hip Thrust #9 . . . . . . . . . . . . . . . . . . . . . . 100
Bulgarian Split Squat #10 . . . . . . . . . . . . . . . 102

**Upper Body Intermediates . . . . . . . . . . . . . . . . . 104**
Pull Down #11 . . . . . . . . . . . . . . . . . . . . . . 104
Banded Push Up #12 . . . . . . . . . . . . . . . . . . . 106
One Arm Shoulder Press #13 . . . . . . . . . . . . . . 108
One Arm Row #14 . . . . . . . . . . . . . . . . . . . . 110

**Mid Body Intermediates . . . . . . . . . . . . . . . . . . 112**
Bend Over #15 . . . . . . . . . . . . . . . . . . . . . . 112
Banded Dead Bug #16 . . . . . . . . . . . . . . . . . . 114
Banded Plank Walk #17 . . . . . . . . . . . . . . . . . 116

**Chapter 6:** Resistance Training for Special Conditions . . . . . . . . . . . . . . . . 120

Injury Recovery and Seated Workouts . . . . . . . . 120
Recovery Band Exercises for Injuries . . . . . . . . . 121
Immediate Action . . . . . . . . . . . . . . . . . . . . . . . . 121
Get It Checked . . . . . . . . . . . . . . . . . . . . . . . . . . 122
Go Lighter in Resistance. . . . . . . . . . . . . . . . . . . . 123

**Seated Resistance Band Exercises . . . . . . . . . . . 124**

Pointed Toes #18 . . . . . . . . . . . . . . . . . . . . . . . 126
Leg Lift #19 . . . . . . . . . . . . . . . . . . . . . . . . . . . 128
Leg Press #20 . . . . . . . . . . . . . . . . . . . . . . . . . 132
Hip Opening #21 . . . . . . . . . . . . . . . . . . . . . . . . 134
Abdominal Lean #22 . . . . . . . . . . . . . . . . . . . . . 136
Chest Press #23 . . . . . . . . . . . . . . . . . . . . . . . . 138
Shoulder Press (Upwards) #24 . . . . . . . . . . . . . 140
Triceps Extension (v.1) #25 . . . . . . . . . . . . . . . . 142
Triceps Extension (v.2) #26 . . . . . . . . . . . . . . . 144
Biceps Curl (v.1) #27 . . . . . . . . . . . . . . . . . . . . 146
Biceps Curl (v.2) #28 . . . . . . . . . . . . . . . . . . . . 148
Chest Stretch #29 . . . . . . . . . . . . . . . . . . . . . . . 150

**Chapter 7:** Advanced Resistance Band Exercises. . 153

Stepping up to the Challenge . . . . . . . . . . . . . . . 153
A Few Cautions . . . . . . . . . . . . . . . . . . . . . . . . . 154

**Eight Advanced Movements . . . . . . . . . . . . . . . . 155**

Pull To Face #30 . . . . . . . . . . . . . . . . . . . . . . . . 155

Front Squat #31 . . . . . . . . . . . . . . . . . . . . . . . . . 158
Single Leg Deadlift #32 . . . . . . . . . . . . . . . . . . . . 160
Clean and Press #33 . . . . . . . . . . . . . . . . . . . . . . 162
Bear Crawl #34 . . . . . . . . . . . . . . . . . . . . . . . . . 164
Chest Crossover #35 . . . . . . . . . . . . . . . . . . . . . . 167
Resistance Crunch #36 . . . . . . . . . . . . . . . . . . . . 170
Lateral Raise #37 . . . . . . . . . . . . . . . . . . . . . . . 173

**Chapter 8:** Bodyweight Calisthenics and Aerobics . . 176

Getting Even Stronger and Conditioned . . . . . . 176

**Bodyweight Calisthenics . . . . . . . . . . . . . . . . . . . . 178**

Push Ups #38 . . . . . . . . . . . . . . . . . . . . . . . . . . 178
Planks #39 . . . . . . . . . . . . . . . . . . . . . . . . . . . 182
Crunch #40 . . . . . . . . . . . . . . . . . . . . . . . . . . . 184
Leg Raises #41 . . . . . . . . . . . . . . . . . . . . . . . . . 185
Squats #42 . . . . . . . . . . . . . . . . . . . . . . . . . . . 188
Aerobic Exercises . . . . . . . . . . . . . . . . . . . . . . . 190
Aerobic Selection . . . . . . . . . . . . . . . . . . . . . . . 190
Your Aerobic Heart Rate . . . . . . . . . . . . . . . . . . . 191

**Chapter 9:** A Top Athlete Tells You How . . . . . . . . 195

Learn From a Senior Who's Still Playing Tough . . 195
Warming Up . . . . . . . . . . . . . . . . . . . . . . . . . . . 196

**A Full-Body Workout . . . . . . . . . . . . . . . . . . . . . . . 197**

Tom Brady and You . . . . . . . . . . . . . . . . . . . . . . 197
Standing Row #43 . . . . . . . . . . . . . . . . . . . . . . . 198
Banded Push Ups #44 . . . . . . . . . . . . . . . . . . . . 200

Core Rotations #45 . . . . . . . . . . . . . . . . . . . . . . 202
Biceps Curl 46 . . . . . . . . . . . . . . . . . . . . . . . . . . 204
Triceps Extension #47 . . . . . . . . . . . . . . . . . . . . 206
Banded Deceleration Lunges #48 . . . . . . . . . . . 208
Shoulder Press #49 . . . . . . . . . . . . . . . . . . . . . . 210
X-Band Squat #50 . . . . . . . . . . . . . . . . . . . . . . . 211

**Chapter 10:** Safety Tips, Good Practices, a Healthy Diet . . . . . . . . . . . . . . . . . . . 214

Putting More Life in Your Years; More Years in Your Life. . . . . . . . . . . . . . . . . . . . . . 214
Protect Your Joints: Safety Tips for Exercising as a Senior. . . . . . . . . . . . . . . . . . . . . . 215
Good Practices for Seniors . . . . . . . . . . . . . . . . . 217
What About Diet? . . . . . . . . . . . . . . . . . . . . . . . . 220
The Mediterranean Diet . . . . . . . . . . . . . . . . . . . 221
The DASH Diet . . . . . . . . . . . . . . . . . . . . . . . . . . 224
You've Made It! . . . . . . . . . . . . . . . . . . . . . . . . . . 225

**Chapter 11:** Workout Programs . . . . . . . . . . . . . . . . . . 227

Exercise Videos. . . . . . . . . . . . . . . . . . . . . . . . . . 227

**4 Week Workouts. . . . . . . . . . . . . . . . . . . . . . . . . . 228**
Beginner Workout (4 weeks) . . . . . . . . . . . . . . . 229
Intermediate Workout (4 weeks) . . . . . . . . . . . . 232
Advanced Workout (4 weeks) . . . . . . . . . . . . . . 236
Seated Workouts (4 weeks) . . . . . . . . . . . . . . . . 240

**Chapter 12:** Conclusion . . . . . . . . . . . . . . . . . . . . . . 244

The Great Equalizer . . . . . . . . . . . . . . . . . . . . . . . 244

Spread the Word . . . . . . . . . . . . . . . . . . . . . . . . . 247

To leave a review: . . . . . . . . . . . . . . . . . . . . . . . . 249

For Seniors 50, 60 and Beyond . . . . . . . . . . . . . . . 250

Glossary. . . . . . . . . . . . . . . . . . . . . . . . . . . . . . . 252

References. . . . . . . . . . . . . . . . . . . . . . . . . . . . . 257

# FOREWORD

**Exercise is an effective way to maintain and improve physical and mental health, regardless of age.**

It is important to recognize that seniors, like any other demographic, have varying fitness levels. You may be just starting out or a seasoned athlete with many years of training behind you. This book is written for all levels, from beginners to advanced.

If this is your first time exercising in a while, or if you're dealing with an illness, don't worry if you cannot do all the exercises in the book.

If you're a beginner, don't expect to be able to do all the exercises right away—take it slow, and work your way up.

The same goes for intermediates—look to the advanced exercises as motivation to continue your fitness journey, but only move on to them when you're ready.

If you're more advanced, use the full range of exercises in the book as a way to mix up your routine and stay motivated. When planning workouts do not feel obliged to only include advanced exercises.

Find a workout routine that works for you, and stick to it, consistency is the key. Above all, remember that your health is the most important thing, and any exercise you do is a step in the right direction.

If you enjoy this book and it helps you achieve your goals, as I most definitely trust it will, please take a minute to leave a short Amazon review. Your feedback will help others considering starting their fitness journey.

**SCAN TO LEAVE AMAZON REVIEW**

# INTRODUCTION

*Physical fitness is not only one of the most important keys to a healthy body, it is the basis of dynamic and creative intellectual activity.*

John F. Kennedy

## What if There Were a Way for You to Become Stronger?

With the recognition that physical fitness can equate with mental fitness, what if there were an enjoyable, effective way to build strength and endurance, resulting in an improvement to your overall health as you grow older; a convenient, inexpensive, simple form of exercise that:

- Has no need for dumbbells, barbells, kettlebell weights, or exercise machines?
- Does not require expensive equipment or a gym membership?

- Can be performed at home, at work, or just about anywhere?
- Is safe to perform at any age, yet provides the same benefits of weightlifting workouts without the risks?

## *Resistance Band Training*

Resistance Bands are the new alternative to traditional weight training workouts. This method of exercise is quickly growing in popularity for good reason – these bands are easily accessible, portable, and cost effective. Resistance bands are made of stretchable rubber and/or latex materials and are readily available in varying levels of resistance; they are emerging in popularity as the new alternative to achieving optimal fitness levels, regaining lost muscle mass, building strength, and increasing endurance. Seniors are discovering they can become healthier as they attain physical fitness levels they once thought were out of reach.

Resistance bands are proving to be the preferred bodybuilding and strengthening option for anyone, but especially for seniors, because they can be performed at home or just about anywhere; they don't require a gym membership or expensive equipment, and best of all, they really give the results you want – with less risk of injury:

- Safety needs to be a priority when seniors are working out, because muscles and ligaments are less flexible, and more subject to pu ls and strains.
- Balance is another concern, and working with heavy weights can cause falls as well as strains. Resistance bands reduce the potential for injury that is common in traditional weight workouts and those that involve a lot of jumping.

In the following 10 chapters, you'll be instructed on how to use these bands to their full advantage, with a comprehensive list of beginner to advanced exercises along with programs for every level of fitness, safety tips to prevent training injuries, and more.

## In this book, you'll learn:

1. **How resistance bands work:** In Chapter 1, you will be introduced to the concept of using these stretchable bands to achieve the level of resistance appropriate for your level of fitness in order to challenge your muscles as effectively as possible. Just as lifting heavy weights puts a strain on various muscle groups, resistance bands can do the same, resulting in the positive type

of cellular-level damage required to stimulate muscle tissues to rebuild bigger and stronger. Here you will learn why resistance bands are safer than traditional workouts for everyone, but especially for seniors whose muscles, joints, and connective tissues are more susceptible to strains, pulls, tears, and other injuries.

2. **The benefits of this style of training:** Chapter 2 will delve deeper into the benefits of resistance training, and why it's an essential part of preparing for your senior years. You may not realize that a good resistance training program goes beyond preventing injuries, helping to protect your joints and bones, and even improve balance, making you less susceptible to falls. You'll not only look and feel better, but you'll also enjoy a higher level of fitness, resulting in an overall improved quality of life.
3. **Resistance band basics:** In Chapter 3, the world of resistance bands will be opened up to you, so you can understand what types of bands you need, and for what each type is designed. These amazingly simple tools come in a variety of colors – usually to designate varying levels of resistance – and you'll be pleased to know that they are widely available online, and in the many retail stores where you can also find yoga mats and exercise balls. You'll also

be impressed to learn just how inexpensive a set of these bands are!

4. **How to jumpstart your workout:** The first round of basic resistance band exercises will be presented in Chapter 4, which is devoted to beginners. I'm sure you're anxious to get going, and this is the best place to start, especially if you are new to working out, or have let a few too many years slip by since you last did any cardio, did a round of pushups and crunches, or hit the gym. Are you ready to make up for lost time? This chapter will be your jumpstart. Start light, and push the resistance levels as you feel able. Be careful not to overdo it: as a senior, your responses and recoveries will be slower. Take it easier than you feel like in the very beginning to avoid injury and avoid overly sore muscles, both of which will decrease motivation to stick with your new fitness routine in the long-term. Just Temper your ambition with patience, and you will reap the rewards.
5. **Intermediate level exercises:** In Chapter 5, we raise the level with some more challenging exercises. Are you ready to tighten those abdominals and bring back that lost six-pack? Or do your upper arms need some work to get those biceps and triceps in better shape? Maybe you need to strengthen your core and

back muscles to improve your posture, and there's a good chance your lower body—quadriceps, hamstrings, shins, calves, and ankles—could use some constructive work.

6. **Advanced resistance training:** When you are ready to face the challenge, Chapter 6 will familiarize you with the more advanced resistance band exercises. Use sound judgment, and wait to try the advanced movements until you are comfortable with the beginner and intermediate level movements, and are able to safely and comfortably perform 2 to 3 sets of each of those with at least a medium level of resistance.
7. **Tips for those with special conditions:** Many of you may have certain conditions that require more customized resistance training. These are the specialized resistance exercises for when you are recovering from injury, or if you can't comfortably perform resistance training while standing; alternatives that are done while you are seated, and which offer the same benefits of muscle development and increased strength and mobility as their standing versions.
8. **Calisthenics and aerobics:** To round out your complete fitness program, you can supplement your resistance band training with bodyweight

calisthenics and aerobics. These are two forms of exercise that will increase your overall level of physical fitness, both improving cardiovascular conditioning and increasing strength. Plus, adding variation to your workouts can help prevent boredom, reduce the risk of injuries, and potentially increase the frequency and consistency of your workouts over the long term.

9. **A top athlete's routine:** Discover a highly effective resistance band routine that you can easily learn and practice. This is the workout that Tom Brady uses to maintain the peak level of fitness that allows him to still be a winning National Football League quarterback well into his 40s. This routine works for Tom, and will also work for you.

10. **Extras including safety tips and diet:** Chapter 10 will cover how to protect and strengthen your joints, and reduce pain throughout your body. Then, in the spirit of the *Hippocratic Oath's* 'First, do no harm,' (North, 2012), there will be a summary of safety tips that will help prevent injuries, and enable you to make your fitness program a part of your daily routine, putting more years in your life, and more life in your years.

## What about diet?

Yes, what you eat (and how much) is essential to health and fitness, and we'll give you the lowdown on some healthy foods that most experts agree on. I'll be recommending healthy, delicious foods, so you can ignore all those fad diets, and go with the one that will help you live the longest and, most importantly, enjoy the best quality of life possible, so you can feel and perform at peak levels even during your later years.

### *Meet the Author*

Who am I? Well, I'm a Personal Trainer and proud to say I've been studying and practicing physical training for most of my life and can appreciate the benefits this conditioning has done for my own health, not to mention many others whom I have trained so they were able to benefit from this same training and health information. Following are a few notes and quotes to give you a quick overview of my background and experiences, so I can let you know how to start, improve, and finally become an expert in order to achieve a better quality of life, benefiting from my knowledge, and this new exercise method, the benefits of which numerous academic studies have verified, that continues to grow in popularity.

- A fitness nut since my days at UCLA cross-fit, trail running, and skiing are still my passions. During the last 25 years as a Ski Instructor and Personal Trainer, I've trained people of all ages and abilities to achieve their fitness goals. A couple of years ago my father required assistance to improve his health, having become increasingly sedentary with each passing year. It took a sustained effort to get him to accept that it's never too late to get fit, certainly not at just 65 years of age!
- I guided my father through a simple yet progressively challenging home exercise program, and introduced him to healthier eating habits appropriate for his stage of life and individual body type, also taking into account his specific needs due to a medical condition. Today, he lives a fulfilling, active Californian lifestyle, regularly beating me on the golf course.
- Another source of inspiration for me is George Jedenoff. He's the oldest living graduate of Stanford Graduate School of Business (GSB) and was still skiing Snowbird at the age of 103. George attributes a daily exercise program and a positive mindset for this vitality, "***That's why I'm still here because I've been adaptable and optimistic all my life".*** If you get a moment,

watch George's video it is inspirational. He celebrated his 105th birthday in July 2023, and hopes to get at least a couple of days skiing this season at a lower altitude resort than Snowbird. The link and QR code below are to George's video where he shows his daily workout routine. Please take a look, I'm sure you will find it inspirational!

**SCAN FOR VIDEO**

- Through extensive research, teaching many different forms of exercise over my 25-year coaching career, and working with trainers and specialists both in the USA and Europe, I've become an authority on the latest workouts and lifestyle habits that will allow anyone, especially seniors, to learn and adopt effective, efficient, and safe fitness routines. Routines that will give positive results, both mentally and physically, building slowly to ensure you can follow a sustainable and consistent fitness routine that can be continued for life.

What sets this book apart from other strength and fitness guides is that I use my expertise and experience to describe each exercise in detail, so you can easily understand them and follow along at your own pace. I promise to keep it simple, but I also carefully explain the movements and positions with sufficient detail so you can perform each exercise correctly and avoid injury. As part of my promise to you, each exercise in the book is not only illustrated but accompanied by a QR Code, scan it on your mobile to see a video clip of that specific exercise being performed correctly.

My goal is to make complex subjects easy for the rest of us to understand.

Imagine your life with fewer injuries or pain, greater strength, increased endurance, and better overall health. Imagine how good you will look and feel, knowing you are in the best shape you can achieve. I'm excited to share this knowledge with you now, and help you improve your quality of life. Let's get started with Chapter 1!

CHAPTER 1

# Resistance Band Basic Workouts

*I think exercise tests us in so many ways: Our skills, our hearts, our ability to bounce back after setbacks, and it can serve us all well as adult athletes.*

Peggy Fleming

Olympic Champion Skater

## Safely Benefitting and Building Every Part of Your Body

*It's all about resistance*—physical resistance, that is—when it comes to building muscles, strengthening joints, protecting your bones from breaking, improving your posture and balance, and overall, making you look and feel better about yourself. There are other important components to being able to achieve your state of fitness; notably bodyweight calisthenics, cardiovascular (aerobic) conditioning, and following a healthy diet. We'll get to those subjects later on, but the focus now is on resistance training with stretchable bands and tubes.

This is your orientation to learning how to correctly, safely, and effectively use various types of stretchable bands and tubes to achieve the resistance you need to challenge your muscles. Resistance bands have a few terms—you may also hear the terms 'exercise bands' or 'fitness bands.'

As mentioned in the Introduction, just as lifting heavy weights puts a strain on various muscle groups, resistance bands can be used to achieve a similar effect, resulting in the same tearing down of muscle tissues at the microscopic cellular level, followed by a period of rest to permit the amino acids, peptides, and proteins present in your body to rebuild the damaged muscles, making them bigger and stronger. Your muscles don't care how you achieve the resistance, as long as it's performed correctly, and increases gradually in intensity, allowing them sufficient time to rebuild.

Importantly, using resistance bands is safer than weightlifting, *especially for seniors*, whose muscles, joints, and connective tissues have less strength and flexibility and are therefore more susceptible to strains, pulls, tears, and other injuries.

## *The Basics*

Resistance bands are an easy way to introduce yourself to strength training. You can start at a very low resistance level (if desired) and gradually increase the resistance as you build your strength. Whether you are recovering from injury or building muscle strength, there are bands for every level of physical strength.

Resistance bands are pieces of rubber that form flat loops or thin tubes with handles on each end. Personally I find loop bands are easier to use for total body exercises, but regular flat bands can be just as effective, and may be less expensive than tubes which generally have handles to grip. When it comes to flat bands, you simply grasp them, or wind the ends around your hands for an improved grip. You may also connect one end of a resistance band or tube to a fixed object; we'll get to that in a moment.

Resistance bands and tubes are generally sold in sets and are available in increasing levels of resistance depending on the thickness of the band, and its length. Some sports specialty stores may have long lengths of the flat bands on rollers, which can be cut to customized lengths.

"Using resistance bands helps you build your muscle strength and lowers your risk of injury," advises WebMD 2022, citing the versatility of the bands, which can be used to target any desired body part. They help target weight loss, build leg and core strength, and open up your range of movement to advance to other forms of exercise.

## *How the Bands Are Used*

You will typically be using flat resistance bands in several ways; don't be concerned about the following simple examples, because all resistance exercises will be explained, step-by-step, in later chapters:

- **Using only your hands:** the bands are stretched apart, then slowly returned to the starting position. Imagine a simple overhead stretch where you pull the band apart over your head while gripping the right and left ends of the band. Pause for a moment in this position, then allow the band to contract back to the starting position, for 1 repetition in a series. Now think of doing the same thing across your chest—do you see the similarity in movement to working out with weights and machines?

- **Using one of your hands plus a stationary (unmoving) object:** that the band is attached to, so that you are able to pull and stretch the band away from the object, which might be a doorknob or the leg of a heavy table that you've tied one end of the band to. Imagine standing at a right angle to the doorknob, and stretching the band across your chest as far as you are able, pausing, then letting the band contract back to its starting position. This is similar to pulling on the cables of an exercise machine.
- **Using both of your hands plus a stationary object:** that the band is dependent upon; so for example, you can pull up or pull down with both hands at the same time. Picture looping the band over the *top of a door,* so that you can pull down on the bands to create the kind of resistance you'd experience doing pull-ups, chin-ups, or on a pull-down machine at a gym. Similarly, the band can be looped *under the door* to allow you to pull and stretch it upwards, mimicking the movements of barbell or dumbbell curls to build your biceps. *Variation:* Instead of looping the band under a door, you can stand on the middle of the band to hold it as you pull and stretch it upwards with both arms.

It's the same effect: Your biceps will strengthen just as they would with dumbbells!

"You can hold a band in one hand, two hands, loop it around a pole, tie it around your knees or ankles, step on one side, and more," according to a conditioning and strength specialist at New York City's Hospital for Special Surgery. This method is *even better* than using free weights (dumbbells, for example). Jason, a trainer from *Silver Sneakers* (2022) says, "Resistance bands provide more and more resistance as you progress through any given movement. The tighter you pull it, the 'heavier' it gets."

**A note of caution:** Before we go further, let's pause for a moment to underscore the importance of not allowing the resistance bands or tubes to come loose or slip off whatever they are attached to, or are dependent upon, as in the above examples. Be careful as well not to damage the bands by looping them over rough or sharp objects.

How do you determine which kinds of resistance bands or tubes to purchase and use? Since each of us has our preferences, it's best if you try out the different types of bands and tubes before deciding which type to go with, in order to determine which is the most comfortable for you. Flat stretch bands are found to be more versatile than tubes for some people, while others prefer the handles that the tubes usually have, making gripping easier.

In Chapter 3, we'll go much deeper into the various types of resistance bands and tubes you can select.

## Benefits of Resistance Bands

The benefits of resistance band training extend to the gains you'd expect from more traditional forms of resistance workouts, so you should not feel that you're missing out, or that resistance bands are a poor substitute. Consider this:

Tom Brady, the legendary quarterback whose professional football career continued into his 40s, retiring for the second and final time in February 2023, advocates a full body workout routine based entirely on resistance bands. His basic resistance band exercises will be shared with you later in the book.

A quick overview of the benefits which I'll elaborate on further in the next chapter:

- **Increased overall physical strength**, from your neck and shoulders down through your arms, chest, abs and core, legs, ankles, and feet. These gains will be accompanied by an increase in muscle mass if the exercises are sufficiently challenging to your muscles, and if you continue your resistance training over time.

- **Improved posture and balance**, as your back and central body core muscles are stretched and strengthened. These muscles are often weakened by the bad posture we assume by leaning over our smartphones, tablets, and laptops, from sitting too long, and not exercising or walking enough.
- **Increased blood flow and circulation**, resulting from the demands made on your tensioned muscles, requiring your heart to pump more oxygen-rich blood to meet the needs of every muscle cell, and the needs of connective ligaments and tendons. We associate improved circulation with aerobic exercises, but resistance workouts also contribute a meaningful addition.
- **Increased joint and bone strength and health**. Your joints can be the weak or strong point in your body; you have the opportunity with resistance training to strengthen the muscles and connective tissues that will prevent your joints from weakening as you age. The same goes for your entire skeletal system: Strong muscles and connective tissues give your bones the support they need to reduce porosity and prevent breakage.

- **Enhanced mental health and mood** comes from knowing you are taking the effort to be strong and physically healthy, and that you are consciously being proactive in your self-protection. You further benefit from the release of the 'feel good' beta endorphins, which are hormones that come into play following a good resistance or cardiovascular workout. You'll enjoy what's often known as the 'runner's high' for hours.

Inevitably, the question of *increased longevity* arises—will a long-term resistance training program add more years to your life? The answer depends on the combined effect of other factors: cardiovascular conditioning, a healthy diet, abstention from smoking, maintaining a normal weight, management of stress, and lifestyle activities including social interaction are among the most frequently identified factors.

Your genetic profile will have influence, of course, but the most positive approach is to do the best you can with what you have. Of all the actions you have control over, beginning and sustaining a good resistance training program is one of the easiest to take, and one of the most beneficial. Resistance bands and tubes are what makes it easy.

## *Best for Seniors*

When given a choice of resistance training alternatives, age plays a definite role in the selection. Among young adults, generally anything goes, because there's greater flexibility, faster response times to grow muscles, and faster recovery times when there's a strain or pull. So weightlifting, which is potentially the most demanding—and most risky—is a viable option for them.

But once we're out of our 20s and 30s, our bodies' needs and abilities start to change, and our response and recovery times are not as fast or assured as when we were younger. Naturally, as we enter our 50s and 60s, it's a new ballgame altogether, with aches and pains showing up uninvited; that is, even without the challenges and stresses of resistance training.

These are the times to become more careful. And if you are already into your 70s or beyond, your cautions must be even greater. Try doing more repetitions with lighter resistance levels, rather than a few reps of a level that may cause strains. Don't be discouraged; you have every right to perform resistance exercises at any age, but recognize the risks, and don't take unnecessary chances.

In other words, focus on resistance bands as your go-to form of resistance training. You can begin your training with minimal resistance, and there's no chance of dropping a heavy weight on yourself.

There's also an opportunity to improve your balance as you learn the correct form and posture for resistance band exercises. Compare that to the increased risks of losing your balance and falling while lifting weights.

Finally, as a senior, you probably have little interest in having to go to a gym or fitness center, and paying for it! Nor do you want to invest in a set of weights and have them cluttering up your home. Resistance bands are inexpensive, and you can put the entire set in a dresser drawer and still have room for your socks and underwear.

## *Get Checked Out*

This chapter, and most others, include a recommendation to see your doctor or medical professional before beginning an exercise program, especially if you are new to this, and have not worked out in some time.

This applies whether you are planning to conduct resistance or cardiovascular exercises, or ideally, both. You may feel okay, and think you're up to any physical challenge, but you never know what surprises your body may have waiting for you. Let the doctor check you out and clear you for whatever level of working out is medically appropriate for your particular condition.

- If you can't see the doctor before you begin training, play it safe and go slowly using minimal resistance at first. You'll not only benefit by preventing strains or injuries, but you will also find the exercises enjoyable, rather than difficult and enduring. As suggested above, doing more reps with low resistance is less risky than a few reps with greater resistance levels.
- Remember, resistance and other forms of physical training are for the long haul; they are marathons, not sprints. So resist the temptation to push hard and fast. It will pay off generously down the road. And don't forget to see your doctor!

## *What About Pain?*

Any pain that occurs while you are exercising should be taken seriously, especially if it's chest pain. If you feel pain, slow down and see if it goes away; if so, you can continue the exercise at a slower pace, or with less resistance. If the pain persists, stop the exercise, and let your doctor know.

Sometimes it's hard to distinguish pain that's concerning from the discomfort you may feel when you've maximized an exercise, and your muscles are letting you know 'hey, that's enough.' A sharp pain is generally an indication that something's not right and you need to stop immediately. This is different from that feeling your muscles give you when they've been maxed out, and signal that you're reaching your limit of exhaustion.

Don't be influenced by the outdated maxim, "No pain, no gain." Pain is a warning that you need to be attentive to.

## The Benefits

We've given you an overview on the benefits of resistance training; now in Chapter 2, you will take a deep dive into the science of resistance band training, gain an understanding of the amazing things your body can do, and how your workouts will transform you.

## CHAPTER 2

# Benefits of Resistance Band Workouts

*Take care of your body. It's the only place you have to live.*

Jim Rohn

entrepreneur and motivationalist

## Look Better, Feel Better, Be Better

Let's take a dive into the science and facts behind the benefits of resistance training, and why you as a senior (or soon-to-be senior) should make your workout program an essential part of preparing for your body's currently changing needs, as well as for what's to come.

You may not realize that an effective resistance band training program goes beyond building and strengthening your muscles; it can also aid in preventing injuries, and actually improve your skeletal structure by increasing bone density through firming up the support of your bones as it also strengthens your joints.

Training with resistance bands will also increase your stamina and endurance, help you lose weight, and even help increase your sense of balance so you'll be less susceptible to falls.

Become the best you can be! You'll not only look better and feel better, but you'll also experience the ultimate—a better overall quality of life in your senior years.

## *How Resistance Bands Protect Your Skeleton*

Strength training with resistance bands has been found to help keep your bones strong by increasing calcium and magnesium levels in the body, thus making these essential structural elements for our bones. As a result, these weight-bearing activities contribute to increased bone density, thus preventing or reducing osteoporosis, a leading cause of broken bones among both senior men and women.

As health and fitness editor Robert A. Lyon reports in *Senior Fitness* (2022), workouts with bands can isolate and target every muscle in your body. They're portable so you can do them at home or anywhere else you have enough space, making them ideal for "inclusion into your fitness routine on the go," thus making resistance bands a practical, readily available tool for combating bone loss, bone porosity, and bone breakage.

## *About Osteoporosis*

Osteoporosis is a serious health condition that can cause bones to become weak and porous over time. This condition is characterized by bone loss, and increasing porosity of the bones, making them more fragile and subject to breakage. Although there is no cure for osteoporosis, treatments and lifestyle changes can help improve bone density and decrease the risk of fractures.

## Why Does It Happen?

Osteoporosis is caused by a number of factors that lead to bone loss such as age, exercise practices, genetics, diet composition, and an inability (or unwillingness) to carry out daily activities that engage the muscles.

Bone density tests are generally used to diagnose the symptoms of osteoporosis, notably fragile or broken bones.

Orthopedists often recommend lifestyle modifications that can supplement medications through helping to reduce bone loss in patients with osteoporosis. Along with diet and weight management, those lifestyle changes often include recommendations to begin a safe exercise routine, and resistance bands tend to be part of that regimen.

Furthermore, by strengthening the muscles that support the skeletal structure, the risk of the injured or broken bones is reduced. Consider your muscles as the brick-and-mortar of your body, supporting and protecting the steel girders and rebars that form the structure. The stronger and more energized your muscles are, the better they can hold your bones in place, protect them from strains, and giving them much-needed flexibility.

Practicing strengthening exercises with resistance bands can also improve joint mobility by improving the flexibility and strength of the ligaments and tendons that connect your muscles to your bones.

Resistance bands are a great choice for people who want to add more variety and intensity to their workouts, as well as those with joint pain or other medical conditions that preclude them from performing traditional weight-bearing exercises.

- Furthermore, the National Osteoporosis Foundation advises, "Exercise and a nutritious diet are important for reversing osteoporosis." They recommend that

> "People with osteoporosis should aim to engage in weight bearing exercise (ideally using resistance bands) three times per week for at least 20 minutes each time" (Lyon, 2022).

## ***Research Confirms the Efficacy of Resistance Bands***

In response to the question of whether training with resistance bands effectively builds muscle and increases strength and endurance, the Cleveland Clinic (2022) cites a 2019 research report by the National Institutes of Health (NIH) that confirmed training with resistance bands creates virtually the same gains in strength as when using conventional gym machines and free weights.

This report is convincing, so if you've ever doubted whether resistance bands are equal to free weights and weight machines, the following should give you confidence:

## Methodology

- To answer the question of just how effective resistance bands and tubes are, the NIH determined that a "Systematic review with meta-analysis, comparing resistance bands and tubes with conventional (weightlifting) devices could clarify and quantify the benefits provided by both modes."

- The objective of these studies was to measure the effects of resistance band training compared to weightlifting training on muscular strength, in varying population groups.
- Participants who used bands were matched with those who used weights; this precaution was to prevent bias due to demographics such as gender, age, where they lived, as well as health, and physical condition. This assured that the results, and any differences between resistance techniques, would be due to the type of equipment used, and not be influenced by other factors.
- A total of eight separate studies were selected to be included in the analyses; each compared resistance training using only tubes and bands with resistance training using only weight machines and dumbbells, finding the results were similar "Regardless of complementary training performed concomitantly, provided it was similar for both groups." The single key measurement of the results were the effects on muscular strength as the outcome.

- In total, the eight studies involved 224 individuals of varying ages up to 88 years, located in diverse regions: The studies were conducted in separate locations, including the U.S., France, Brazil, Spain, and Australia.
- All studies were among people who were already in the habit of performing some form of strength training, but whose health varied. "Regarding health, the samples varied from physically active individuals and athletes to individuals with coronary heart disease and moderate COPD (Chronic obstructive pulmonary disease). The duration of training ranged from 4 to 12 weeks, two to five times a week."

## The Results of the Analyses

In summary, the NIH states that "The outcomes of this systematic review and meta-analysis demonstrated that training with elastic resistance provides strength gains similar to training with conventional resistance." In other words, the studies confirmed with statistical confidence that there is "No superiority between training performed with elastic resistance and training with weight machines and/or free weights on strength gain."

## Other studies verify these findings:

- "Systematic reviews with meta-analysis ... demonstrated positive effects on muscular strength gained from the use of elastic resistance when compared with a control group in the elderly and individuals with osteoarthritis and fibromyalgia."

## *Conclusion:*

"Evidence from this study suggests that resistance training with elastic devices provides similar strength gains when compared to resistance training performed with conventional weightlifting devices" (Cleveland Clinic, 2022).

The NIH recommended that these results should encourage physiotherapists, coaches, and trainers to recommend using resistance bands and tubes, which are safe and easy to handle, relatively low in cost, and can be used in the home or workplace to effectively build muscle mass and gain muscular strength and endurance.

## Additional Advantages to Resistance Bands

Cited by the Cleveland Clinic (2022), exercise physiologist Christopher Travers, MS says that "No matter what your fitness level, resistance bands are a great piece of equipment to use. Resistance bands might not look like much, but they can strengthen your muscles as effectively as more traditional weights," he affirms. The bands may even have an advantage in terms of their effectiveness. As Christopher suggests: "In many ways, bands put more tension on your muscles and work them longer during movements."

## Many Weight Lifters Give Up

Weight lifting does not appear to have good staying power among its participants; possibly less continuity than resistance band usage. This suggests there are advantages to the conveniences and unique benefits of resistance bands and tubes. The researchers who conducted the analyses have offered explanations as to why resistance band training may have further advantages over traditional weight lifting practices:

- "Despite the widespread use of conventional devices, such as weight machines and dumbbells, and their results regarding strength gains, it is believed that, on average, 50% of people who adopt this type of training give up during the first year of practice" (NIH, cited by Cleveland Clinic, 2022). No resistance technique can be considered effective if its adherents don't stay with it for the long term.

- This behavior by those who begin resistance training by lifting weights and using weight machines may be traced to factors such as logistical difficulties, financial costs, and the lack of time to head out to the gym, which make the use of weights impractical in many situations.
- Therefore, because resistance band training does not impose these kinds of difficulties, the use of portable bands and tubes allows for greater accessibility, leading to better adherence, at no loss in the quality and results of the exercises!

So, based on these findings, you can confidently begin resistance training with bands and tubes, and stick with these devices over the long term.

## *Why Resistance Bands Are So Effective*

There's an actual physiological advantage to using stretchable bands and tubes, compared with lifting weights. It's called 'accommodating resistance'. This means the farther you pull a resistance band, the greater the degree of resistance it exerts. This is a different and potentially more beneficial form of resistance compared to a dumbbell or barbell, or a machine with cables and weights.

For example, consider when you perform bicep curls:

- As you curl the dumbbells upwards towards your shoulders, "There comes a point where the curl actually gets 'easy' for your biceps, near the top of the motion." The length of the lever that challenges your biceps decreases as you finish the exercise.
- Therefore, the downward pull of gravity is no longer able to challenge your bicep with the dumbbell, and as a consequence "Your muscle no longer needs to create as much force to fight that challenge." What should be the area of peak resistance – the top of the curl – ends up as a moment of minimal resistance.

In contrast, when you perform a similar upward curling movement with a resistance band, the reverse effect occurs:

- "As you near the top, it doesn't get easier; instead, you have to work to earn the squeeze at the top of the curl." As the band stretches, it fights harder, tensing your bicep increasingly throughout the full range of motion, challenging your muscle fibers via a continuous increase in tension.

- *Men's Health* concludes: You'll be sure to feel the optimal resistance at the top of the curl; there's no "slacking off" as with the dumbbell. "You'll have to squeeze your muscles extra-hard to fight banded resistance" (2022).

## Physical Changes You Can Expect

Resistance bands are cited by *BodyGym* (2022) for their effectiveness in improving your posture, increasing blood circulation, reducing the risk of disease, improving mental health including elevating your mood, decreasing the chances of injury during training, and improving balance and mobility.

This is, of course, in addition to helping increase your physical strength and endurance, given that consistent resistance training builds muscle mass.

As confirmed in the NIH meta-analysis discussed above, resistance bands provide similar increases in strength compared to traditional resistance training like weight lifting, with the added benefit of causing increased muscle activation in the ancillary muscles:

- In weight training, and especially for powerlifting, 'ancillary' refers to muscles that support and interact with other muscle groups, including those that help support the main muscles when doing heavy duty lifting during squats (which engage the quadriceps), bench presses (for the chest), and deadlifts (to strengthen the lower back). Training with resistance bands and tubes helps engage these ancillary muscles without using weights.

"Due to the nature of the resistance bands, you will force your muscles to contract faster," reports *BodyGym*, emphasizing that "The constant resistance that you have to work against increases your muscle control when done correctly. The effect is more muscle mass and more significant stability."

## *Consistency Is Key to Results*

It may be tempting to think that you can perform resistance exercises for a brief time, then coast for a while. Perhaps you become satisfied with your physical progress after a month of training, and feel you've earned some time off. But it doesn't work that way.

Unlike the flu and pandemic vaccinations we're all receiving, resistance training is not a one-time shot that will protect you for months or even longer. If you want to continue to grow stronger and increase your endurance, you will need to invest your physical efforts on a continuing, consistent basis. If you don't, your gains will be lost, and the benefits you've earned will diminish.

This does not imply that you should not rest—quite the contrary—since rest is an essential component of effective resistance training. But the rest you need is in days, not weeks or months:

- We've mentioned the process of 'hypertrophy', which occurs when you damage the cells of your muscle fibers during an effective resistance workout, whether it's done with bands or weights. In the 24 to 48 hours that follow, your body undergoes a repair process, with infusions of proteins sent to the damaged muscle fibers. In performing these repairs, there is a small amount of protein overbuilding, which accumulates over time to increase muscle mass, and strength potential.

This is why you do not want to perform resistance exercises using the same muscle groups on consecutive days. If you are a senior, allow at least two days for your muscles to rebuild; possibly even a third day if you feel it's needed. Therefore, you only need three days of resistance training each week to experience maximum benefits.

So what happens when you stop your resistance training, or let too much time pass between workouts? Your muscles will gradually atrophy or diminish in size and strength. Whatever progress you made will be lost. In addition, the psychological benefits from working out—

the sense of satisfaction that comes from the feeling of toned and strengthened muscles, and the feel-good post-workout beta endorphins—will not occur.

It's okay if you miss a day from time to time, but try to get in at least two good workouts with your resistance bands every week.

Finally, be sure to get a *full body workout*, rather than limiting your total conditioning to a limited group of muscles, like arms and shoulders, or your chest and abdominals. Optimal health and fitness is dependent on overall conditioning.

You can achieve this by doing full body workouts, with days of rest in between, or you can work different muscle groups on different days. It's okay, for example, to exercise your upper body on one day, and your lower body the next day. You'll learn more about all of these resistance band exercises in subsequent chapters.

**Equipment:** Let's move on to the types of resistance bands and tubes that you can choose from.

**CHAPTER 3**

# An Introduction to Resistance Bands

*Age is no barrier. It's a limitation you put on your mind.*

Jackie Joyner-Kersee

Olympic track athlete

## Knowing What to Buy and How to Use

It is time to learn about resistance bands and tubes, so you can determine what you need, and what they will do for you. Despite their basic simplicity, bands and tubes come in a variety of colors to indicate levels of resistance, which range from low level beginner's strength to resistance levels that can challenge even the most serious weight lifters. This chapter will help you understand the advantages of the various types, so you won't be overwhelmed by their many advertising and product displays.

Finding where to buy resistance bands and tubes needn't be difficult; there are loads of offers online, from Amazon to smaller suppliers. Many different types of bands and tubes can also be found at sporting goods stores like Dicks, at specialized retailers that also offer other types of exercise equipment such as yoga mats and exercise balls, and even mass retailers like Target, Walmart, and Bed, Bath & Beyond.

Finding the bands and tubes won't be hard, but selecting the ones that best fit your needs may take some research, and searching a few local or online stores. The objective of this chapter is to help with your decision-making.

## *Low Cost and Compact*

You'll appreciate how inexpensive a set of these bands is, especially compared to the monthly costs of a gym or fitness center membership. And as we've mentioned, you can pack them away easily, bring them with you to work, or when traveling.

How much will you pay? As a quick guideline, you can purchase a set of three resistance bands of varying strengths (that is, resistance levels) for about $15, or a single resistance tube with handles for $10-$15. You may want to consider the many kits and more elaborate sets of bands and tubes available at higher prices. These can range in cost from $25-$50 or more, but that's still nowhere near the cost of a full set of weights, benches and racks, which can add up to hundreds of dollars or more.

Consider too the compact size and portability of resistance bands and tubes, compared to the bulk of weights and related equipment. Would you really want to clutter up your home or office with all that bulky iron and steel?

## *Bands, Tubes, or Both? Different Types of Resistance Bands*

There are really just two distinct types of stretchable resistance devices: flat bands, and cylindrical tubes with handles. But there are variations within these two categories, resulting in a total of nine types of bands. For example, flat stretch bands may be straight or looped; the loop makes certain exercises easier to perform but may also limit other uses. Which type you will choose will depend on how you plan to use them, and with which style you are most comfortable.

Following, you'll find the nine band styles described by fitness authority and editor Evan Porter in *Trusty Spotter* (2020). See if you can relate to the types of bands that seem right for you; they range from very low resistance levels for rehab from injuries, to intense resistance for those who are serious about building big muscles and getting much stronger.

As you review these descriptions, and subsequently 'shop' the options online or at retail, you will realize that the bands are mostly interchangeable; that is, a few basic bands can be used to perform a wide range of exercises. One of the most important considerations is being sure you obtain a range of resistance ranges: low, medium, and high.

1. **Therapy bands:** As the name implies, therapy bands are typically used for rehabilitation. Therapy bands are generally lighter in resistance than other bands. If you are recovering from an injury, especially to a limb or a joint, your doctor may recommend these minimal resistance bands to gradually work and strengthen your muscles without the risk of straining the injured area, or making the injury worse. According to personal trainer Allan Misner in

Trusty Spotter (2020), who specializes in training seniors, "These are straight thin elastic bands that provide mild resistance. These are useful for rehabbing an injury as you work to begin rebuilding some basic strength and stability." As with most other bands, you may hold an end in each hand, or attach one end to a sturdy object, or even stand on the band for certain movements. Note that instructions for all types of bands will be coming in subsequent chapters.

2. **Compact bands:** These are bands that are tubular in shape, available either individually, or in a set with varying levels of resistance. These consist of a set of cord-like bands available in varying colors and resistance levels. As with all types of tube-shaped bands, they generally have handles at both ends, or just a handle at one end, plus clips or other anchoring mechanisms that allow you to attach the band to a door or other sturdy object; compact bands may also come with wrist or ankle cuffs. Tubes tend to be longer than flat stretch bands, extending to up to four feet in length. Tubes with plastic handles at one or each end are recommended for training your arms, and upper and lower body. This form of resistance band provides a wide variety of uses, and due to its

versatility, is recommended by many trainers and rehab specialists.

3. **Mini loop resistance bands:** These are comparatively small bands, typically nine to 12 inches in length, that are looped around your thighs, knees, ankles or calves. The idea is to provide resistance as you separate your limbs, creating tension between them. They are cited as the best for tensing the glutes and hips, among other lower body muscle groups. Personal trainer Monica Straight says in Trusty Spotter (2020) that "Mini Bands are my current favorite! They're great for lateral workouts, for maintaining form, and intensifying common exercises like squats." When we perform squats, there's a tendency to let the knees come together, but by using a mini loop, you can remain conscious of the need to keep the knees apart. Another advantage of mini loops is their ease of use compared to holding on to the ends of a flat, straight resistance band.
4. **Figure-eight bands:** As the name says, this is a looped band that is connected in the center to form the shape of a number eight, with handles you can grip. This type of band is reminiscent of spring-based stretchable exercise devices that were once popular. The popularity of figure-eight bands is their

ease of assisting you in performing many functional exercises. For example, they help to isolate specific muscle groups to increase the effectiveness of strength conditioning. You can also find ways to incorporate this type of band into physical therapy, or pilates exercises. For example, to use a figure-eight band to strengthen your abdominal muscles, you would lie back on a mat in a crunch position, and insert one foot into a loop of the band, holding the other loop with the opposite hand. As you pull with your hand and push with your foot, you will feel your abs tensing. You would perform this exercise for a certain number of stretches, then reverse the position to repeat on the other side. Despite their small, compact size and portability, figure-eight bands can be used to work different muscle groups, and they're great for working different muscle groups. I find these particularly useful when traveling, or if time only permits a quick home workout.

5. **Ring resistance bands:** This type of band resembles a chain with links; it's designed to let you alter the width of your grip, which allows you to easily increase or decrease the degree of resistance. Users of ring bands find them extremely versatile, allowing them to target their hands and arms, neck

and shoulders, core and abdominals, joints, thighs, calves, ankles and feet, depending on where they grip the band, and which body part or muscle group they choose to exercise.

6. **Lateral resistance bands:** These are long, flat bands with cuffs on each end that are particularly useful when performing leg exercises. For example, the cuffs facilitate being able to wrap the band around your ankles to perform a movement called 'lateral walk' strength training. This, and other walking exercises with a resistance band, can help you target your hip abductors, and your gluteus maximus and medius (bum) muscles. As an alternative, longer loop bands can also be used for these effects. For example, with the bands attached to your ankles, you can dip down into a half-squat by bending your knees and taking side steps (being careful to not lose your balance!) Walking with bands that constrain your legs can provide a good warmup routine before beginning challenging cardiovascular exercises. The bands help improve stabilization of your knee joints, and increase ankle stability early in your workouts to help prevent strains and injuries.
7. **Pull up bands:** Here is an excellent example of how resistance bands can be used in place of traditional

resistance band exercises: in this case the pull up, which normally requires an elevated horizontal bar. Resistance bands can be used to replicate the full motion and exertion of a real set of pull ups, or can be used at a lower resistance level, to train you to be able to do pull ups later on, as your strength increases. As you will learn, pull up bands can be stretched over a door, enabling you to pull down, providing the equivalent effectivity of a traditional pull up, if the resistance level is sufficient; otherwise, you'll be underachieving the effort. Alternatively, you can use them to assist in a traditional pull up: In a gym or fitness center, you may see a trainer or spotter helping someone do pull ups with a helping upward shove; the resistance bands can play this same role. To perform this function, the resistance band has to be quite long so you can stand on it and extend it to the bar.

8. **Flat resistance bands:** As the name implies, these are simple, flat stretchable bands, without any cuffs, clips or handles. They are simply longer, higher resistance versions of Therapy Bands. They may be purchased in pre-cut lengths, or cut to order from a large roll. If you are cutting to order, be sure the band is long enough for all of the movements you'll be making. Also be sure to get

several bands with differing levels of resistance. Exercises that can be performed with these long flat bands include the chest press, lateral raise, lunges, standing or seated curl, and the standing high row. Using your imagination, most weight lifting movements can be replicated with flat bands, and many bodyweight exercises can be intensified (like squats, pull-ups, and push-ups).

9. **Tube bands:** Unlike flat stretchable bands, tube bands are cylindrical, with the further distinction of having handles at each end, or at least a handle at one end, and a clip for an attachment at the other end. At first look, the tube band with handles may look like a jump rope, but don't underestimate its potential. It makes holding on to the band a cinch, and may potentially facilitate your ability to handle greater resistance than you could with a flat band that doesn't have any grip except for the band itself. Tube bands possess the advantage of acting like a cable pulley you'd find at the gym and dumbbells combined. They are one of the most versatile and useful types of resistance bands available. My advice, if you can only buy one type of resistance band for home use, a set with handles is a great choice. Tube bands with handles may be a bit more expensive than their flat counterparts, but you may find them

easier and more effective to use. As noted earlier, you can acquire a basic set of three flat resistance bands for $15 or less, or to get a complete set of bands and tubes with handles, the costs can range from $25-$50 or more.

Now that you know more about the types of bands available, let's take a look at how and where to purchase them.

## *Where to Purchase*

**Online:** The selection of resistance bands and tubes online is awesome, with hundreds of selections from major retailers like Target and Walmart, to online stores like Amazon, plus many other smaller suppliers.

The upside to buying them online is that you can get information about each offer with a click, and be able to find the best prices.

The downside is the absence of personalized assistance and advice, and having to wait for delivery. Many suppliers offer free, expedited shipping, but make sure you are meeting their minimum payment to qualify. Another downside of online shopping for resistance bands and tubes is the overwhelming selection, making it hard to choose.

Be sure the online vendor offers a satisfaction guarantee, so you can return or exchange your purchase if the resistance bands don't meet your expectations.

**Retail:** If you live or work near a Target, Walmart, Bed, Bath & Beyond or other mass retailer, chances are good their sporting goods section will have a limited supply of resistance bands to choose from. It will be limited because they don't have the room for as extensive selection as they have online, where they can draw from large warehouse inventories.

The good news is you can see and even test the equipment, and hopefully get some advice from store personnel. And there's no waiting for delivery!

If you can get to sports-focused retailers such as Dick's, Big 5, or Paragon, you will find a larger selection, and will most likely have access to more knowledgeable staff to guide you better in your search.

## *Using Your Bands: Some Safety Tips*

You will use your bands or tubes in essentially two ways: holding one end of the band in each hand, or holding one end while the other end is anchored to an immovable object.

**When anchoring:** It's important to be attentive in order to prevent injury to yourself, or damage to the band or tube. If an end is clipped or tied to a doorknob or the leg of a dresser or heavy table, ensure it will not detach under the strain you'll be subjecting it to. You do not want the band snapping back and hitting you, especially in the face!

Similarly, be careful if you are attaching the band to a doorknob or are inserting one end into a dresser drawer. Before starting your workout, double check by pulling hard on the band to ensure it's well-anchored.

If your exercise requires draping or looping the band over a door so you can perform variations of pull ups or chest pull downs, be sure the band is far enough from the edge that it won't slip off. And be sure the top of the door isn't rough enough to cut or abrade the rubber material the band is composed of. You can place a small towel under the band to protect it from abrasion.

Note that it's not advised to try to anchor a tube by hooking one handle on a doorknob or other object, because it can slip off during the movement. This can be even more dangerous than the rubber band hitting you!

**When gripping both ends of the band or tube:** The handles of a tube band make it reasonably sure that you can hang on without trouble, but when you are using a flat band where you're holding onto the rubber stretch band itself, it's a good idea to wrap each end around your hands rather than attempting to clench or squeeze it. Just be aware that wrapping the band like that shortens it and increases its resistance—a good thing to remember when increased tension is desired.

## *Getting Started*

Once you've selected your resistance training bands, you are ready to go! The following chapter will give you a good start with some basic exercises for beginners.

CHAPTER 4

# Beginner Resistance Band Exercises

*First, do no harm.*

Hippocratic Oath

## Enthusiasm Tempered by Caution

If you are a beginner or completely new to working out, and want to start getting bigger, stronger muscles and improving your overall well-being, we'll help you get started in achieving results that will make your investment of time and effort worthwhile.

We especially don't want you to either underachieve and end up discouraged, or to overdo it and injure yourself. Too many well-intended seniors start working out enthusiastically, only to become disappointed waiting for results, or sustaining injuries, leading to a lack of motivation and becoming tempted to quit instead of developing a healthy, positive lifelong exercise habit.

You're now ready for a set of basic exercises that will help you become familiar with using resistance bands. You're probably excited to begin, and this is a good place to start, especially if you are new to working out, or haven't done resistance training with weights, calisthenics, or bands in recent years.

**Know your limits:** As a senior, your responses and recoveries will be slower, so it's recommended that you exercise patience at this point, controlling your ambition to build muscles and grow stronger, so you avoid overdoing it, or causing injuries. As the Hippocratic Oath taken by new doctors reminds us, caution is the best course. While your risks of injury are less than with weight lifting, you can still cause strains, pulls, and tears, or just over-exhaust yourself if you force your body to exceed your current level of ability.

## *Preparation*

**Minimal equipment:** Apart from the resistance bands and tubes, there isn't much equipment needed. Wear sweats, or any light stretchable clothing, so you don't constrain movement or range of motion. If there's any kneeling or lying down involved, use a yoga mat or carpet to protect your joints and back.

The way resistance bands can be used is almost limitless. They can be held in one hand, tied around your knees for side-steps, as mentioned earlier, or securely looped around a pole. These are only some of the possibilities available.

**Unique advantages:** Another advantage compared to free weights, resistance bands provide increasing resistance as you progress through each movement. The tighter you pull it, the greater the bands' resistance and the 'heavier' the movement becomes. This was mentioned previously: A free weight, such as a dumbbell or barbell, gets light at the top of a movement, while resistance bands keep on intensifying the resistance!

Another important benefit unique to resistance bands is enabling you to challenge your muscles from many different angles, which helps you to perform everyday tasks. As you proceed through your day's activities, "You don't just move your arms side to side or your legs up and down. You want to be able to move in a variety of directions," notes Alisha Fetters, C.S.C.S., in *Silver Sneakers*.

## *Warm Up and Breathing*

**Warming up:** Before beginning even a resistance workout, give your body some preliminary exercise and stretching to get your circulation going, helping your heart to start pumping more blood throughout your body:

- Ideally, you will perform a cardiovascular workout before resistance training, for the most complete oxygenation of all your muscles. 5 to 10 minutes on the treadmill or elliptical, or, if working out at home and time is limited, you can do some brisk walking for five to ten minutes, or climb a few flights of stairs.
- Next do some light stretching and yoga movements, such as the cat-cow, sphinx and cobra, pelvic tilt, downward dog, child's pose, seated leg extensions, and some side stretches (if you're not familiar with these yoga moves and poses, a quick lookup online will show you how to perform each pose). Throw in a few squats and a plank for 30 seconds, and you should be ready to go.
- Perform the movements you plan to make with the resistance bands, but without any resistance initially. This will help loosen your muscles and lubricate the joints that will be involved.

- Give your sense of balance a warmup too; this will help reduce the risk of falling. Stand erect, and raise the knee of your right leg until your thigh is parallel to the floor, or as high as you feel comfortable with. You may wish to gently hold the back of a chair or place one hand against a wall. Hold for 10-15 seconds, then lower and repeat with your left leg.

**Breathing:** During the warmup, begin to concentrate on your breathing, since managed breathing will improve the quality of your resistance training, as well as improving your state of mindfulness and inner peace:

- Inhale slowly and deeply, extending your gut outwards. This will expand your diaphragm, enable your lungs to fill with more air, and hence, be able to deliver more oxygen to the blood, and onward to your muscles.
- As you perform each move, exhale slowly and fully, pulling in your gut to contract your diaphragm. It should feel like you are pulling your abs towards your spine. More air will be expelled, and with it, more CO2 and metabolic waste.
- Remain conscious of these deep inhales and exhales, since they will focus your concentration and divert any distressing thoughts—this type

of breathing is practiced during yoga, as well as many types of meditation.

- As you perform each resistance exercise, exhale during the harder part of the movement, and inhale during the easier part. For example, exhale as you raise your hands and forearms in a curl (when the resistance increases), and inhale as you lower (as the resistance decreases).

## ***Reps and Sets***

**Reps:** All forms of resistance training are based on doing a certain number of 'reps', also known as repetitions; the consecutive reps are called a 'set'. So if you do 10 reps without stopping to rest, that's one set of 10 reps.

How many reps you perform in a set depends on the resistance of the bands or weight being lifted. Logically, the lighter the resistance, the more reps you can do and vice-versa; heavier weights or resistance will reduce the number of reps you can perform.

For most situations, there is a consensus among trainers and physiologists that the level of resistance should be what you can lift or pull for 8 to 12 reps in a set before finding it difficult to do more:

- Of course, how much you can lift is entirely a function of your personal condition, so no one should dictate to you to curl 10 reps of a 20 lb weight (or its resistance equivalent).

- Through some testing, you should be able to determine what your starting resistance should be to get to that 8 to 12 rep range.
- If your supply of varying resistance bands is limited, you may find that one level is too low, and the next is too high. In that case, opt for the *lower level* of resistance and do more reps to get to the point of *enough!* In time, you'll grow stronger and be able to move up to the next level of resistance to achieve your 8 to 12 reps.

**Sets:** The standard among noted physiclogists is two to three sets of reps per muscle group workout, with a 40 to 60 second rest between each set. This brief rest period gives your muscles some recovery time, so even though the previous set may have exhausted your muscles, they will bounce back enough for you to start another round:

- Don't be surprised if you find it difficult to do the same number of reps in sets two and three that you performed in the first set. This is a positive sign that you are giving yourself an effective, challenging workout. Try to tough it out, knowing the harder you work, the greater the muscle and strength increases you'll experience. (If you need to, extend your rest time between sets to increase recovery time as is individually necessary.)

- Later in your training, when you have been working out regularly for at least one month, you may also want to try increasing the resistance in the latter sets to further work each muscle group; just be prepared to do fewer reps than in the previous set.
- Finally, remember not to perform resistance workouts with the same muscle groups on consecutive days. Give yourself at least one, or ideally two rest days, to allow for the protein-adding hypertrophy process to rebuild and strengthen your muscle fibers and tissues.

## *Beginner Resistance Band Exercises*

These are a group of resistance exercises which are relatively simple and few in number but can give you a full body workout. These moves come together to form a good starter kit if you are new to resistance training with bands, or if you want a short, manageable group of exercises to begin with.

Always remember to keep good form, since bad posture and slouching will reinforce any tendencies to be bent over (which often happens as we age).

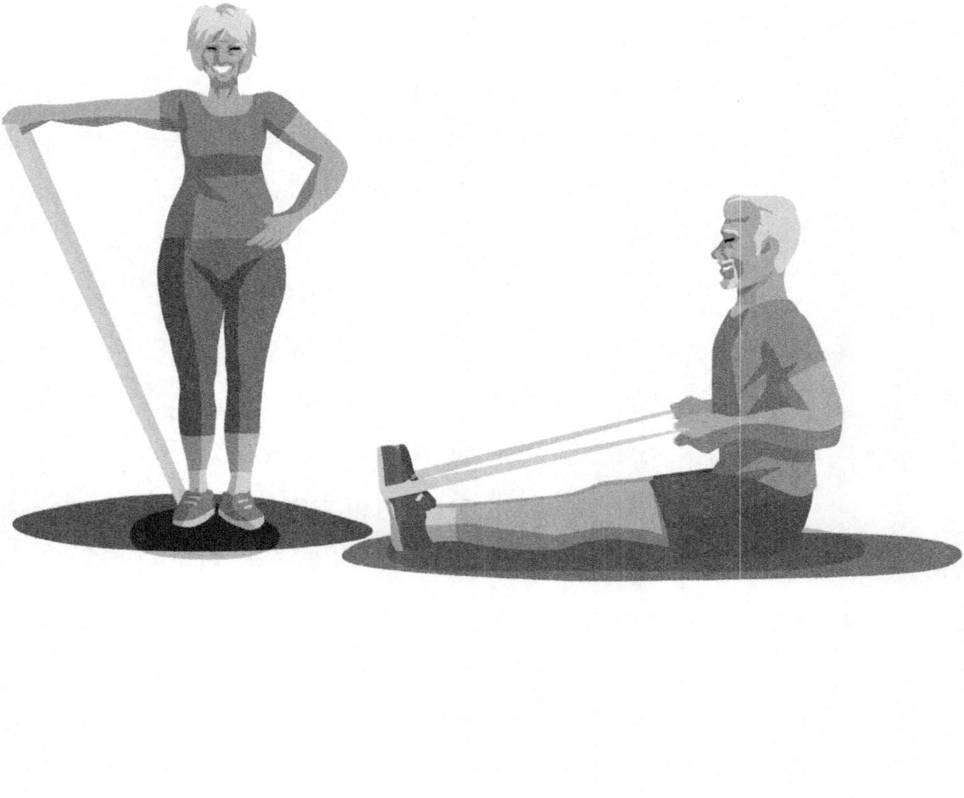

## Chest Pull Apart #1

This move opens your chest and strengthens your pectoral and shoulder muscles, as well as your arms and wrists. Your posture benefits too:

---

- Stand upright, holding one end of the band or tube in each hand. Raise your hands to chest height and about six inches out from your chest. Begin the exercise by pulling the bands apart, keeping your elbows close to your body. The resistance level should be sufficient to feel the tension, but not enough to cause strain or extreme difficulty.
- Try to stretch the band until your hands and forearms are perpendicular to your body, that is, pointing to the sides. If you can, extend the movement by reaching out further to the sides; this will engage your lats and upper back muscles.
- As you reach the peak of the stretch, try to force your shoulder blades apart. Pause then slowly return to the starting position. Perform 10 to 12 reps, rest, and repeat for one or two more sets.

**SCAN FOR VIDEO**

## Lat Pulldown #2

Muscles engaged: The lats (latissimus) that are the muscles just beneath your shoulders and that connect your chest, shoulders, and upper back. This simulates the lat and chest pulldown machine in fitness centers.

---

- Hold a straight (not looped) flat exercise band or tubular band in both hands. Stand erect with your arms raised directly overhead and held shoulder-width apart. Your palms should face forward.
- Create tension in the band by pulling it until it is fully extended, but not yet stretched. Keep the left arm elevated as you slowly lower your right arm, and pull the band apart until your right hand until it's in line with your shoulder.
- Slowly raise your right arm to the starting position and repeat the exercise with your left arm. That makes 1 rep. Or you may do all of the reps with one arm before repeating with the other arm.
- Perform a first set of 8 to 12 reps with each or both arms. Rest for up to 60 seconds, then perform a second set, and a third if you are able.

**SCAN FOR VIDEO**

## Seated Row #3

Rowing machines are used to exercise the upper and lower back, the core, and the shoulders. You will like the feeling of this nearly full body exercise.

---

- Sit in a chair or on a bench with both legs extended, and extend the center of a long band or tube behind the middle of your feet. Hold the ends of the band with each hand, and extend your arms, turned so your palms are facing each other.
- Sit upright (making sure not to bend at the waist), bend your elbows, and pull the band inward, towards your gut. As you reach the peak of the stretch, squeeze your shoulder blades together.
- Return slowly to the starting position and repeat for 10 to 12 reps. Rest for up to 60 seconds, then do a second set.

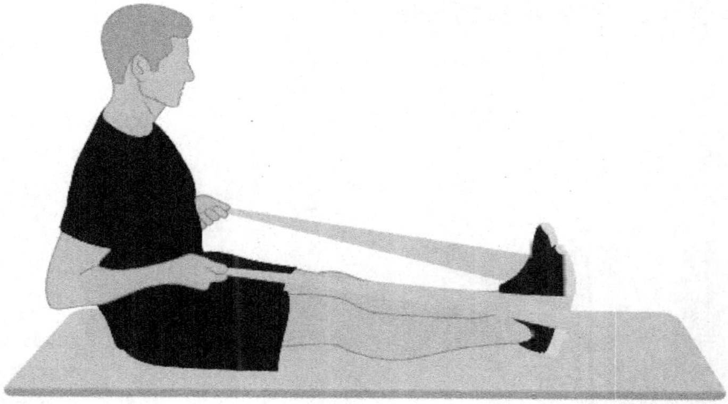

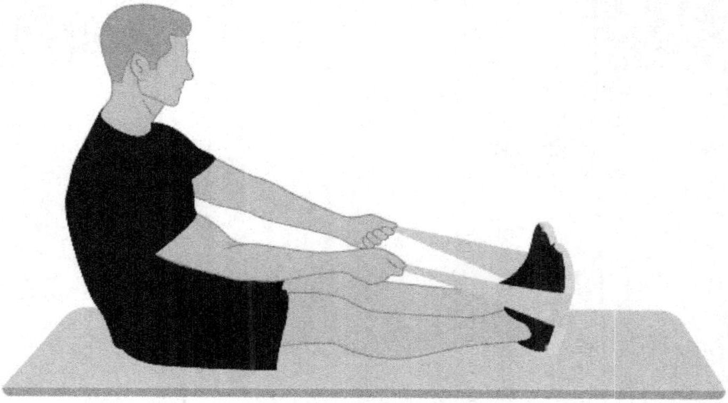

**SCAN FOR VIDEO**

## Modified Seated Row

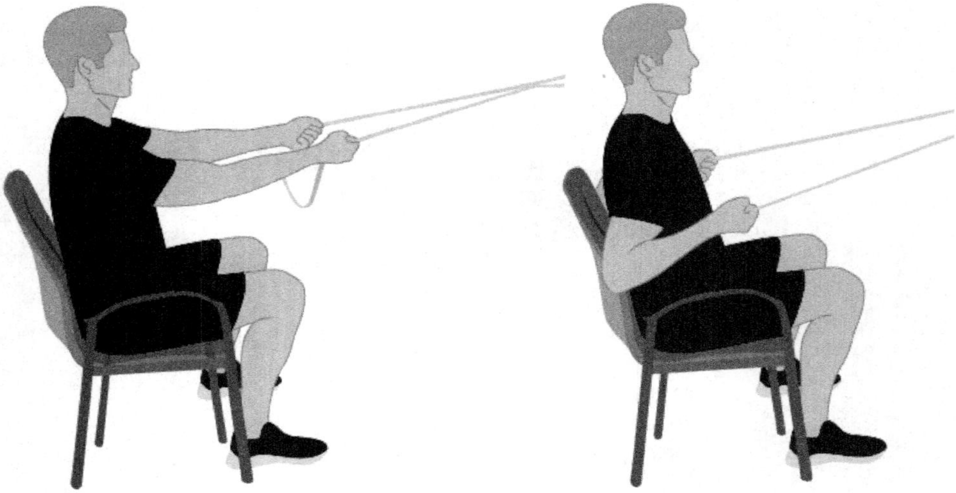

**SCAN FOR VIDEO**

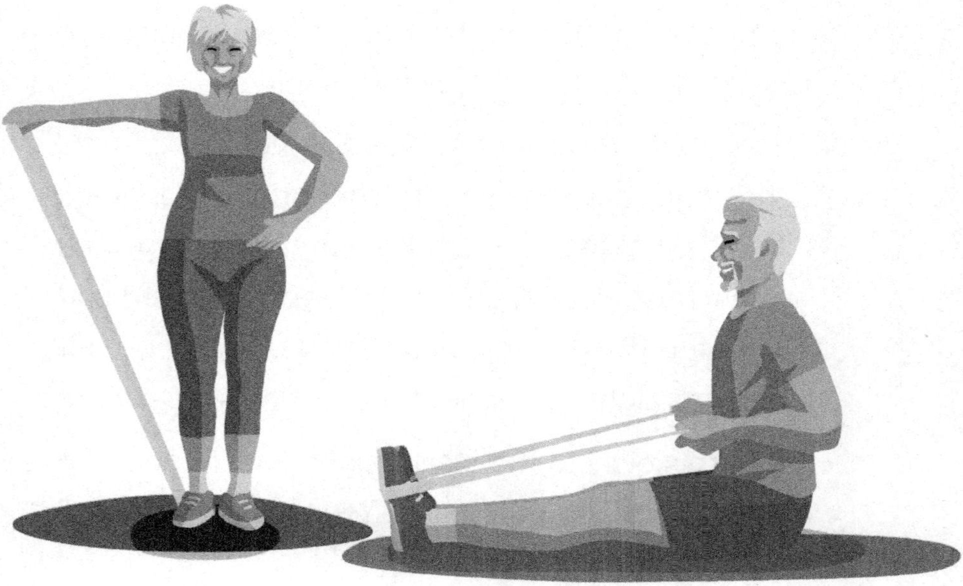

## Pallof Press #4

This is an effective way to improve core stability and help relieve back pain.

---

- Securely wrap the resistance band around a doorknob or other immovable object. Hold the other end of the band with both hands, raised to chest height. Stand facing the object.
- Step backwards (carefully, so as not to trip) until the band is taut. Then turn your body 90 degrees from the object, so it's on your side. Using both arms, push the band or tube directly forward and hold for 15 seconds, making sure to keep your body straight throughout the movement.
- Return slowly to the starting position. Repeat the exercise on the other side. You may do a second round if comfortable.

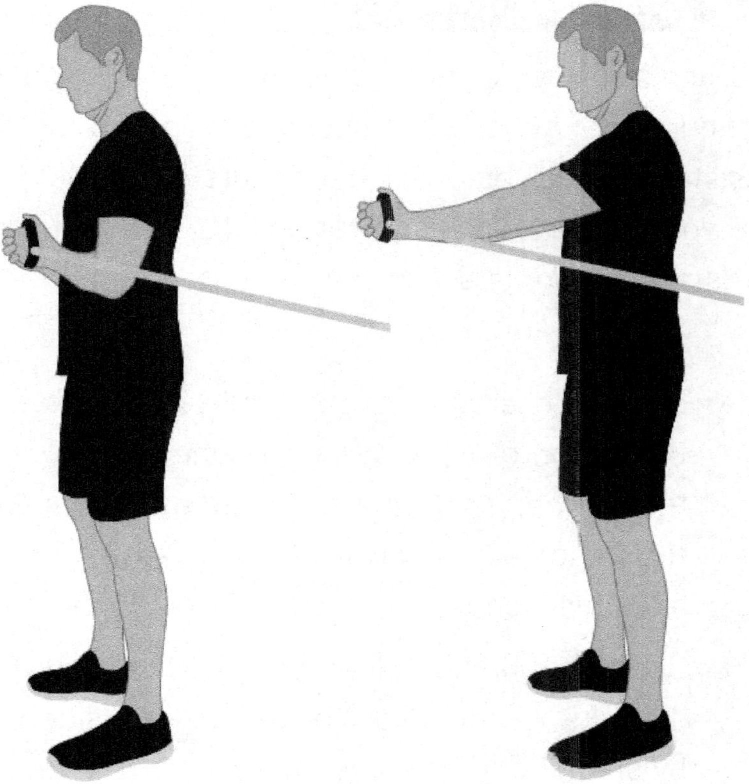

**SCAN FOR VIDEO**

## Band Side Step #5

Walking sideways is good for balance training, but does not build strength, unless, that is, there is some serious resistance involved. Your hip flexors will benefit, as will your glutes, quads and hamstrings, when a looped resistance band gets involved.

---

- Loop an exercise band around your knees, with the option of (1) above your knees for the least resistance; (2) below your knees for medium resistance; or (3) closer to your ankles for the most resistance.
- Bend your knees slightly and place your feet hip-width apart. Now begin to walk sideways by stepping to one side until the band gives you resistance, then slide your rear foot back over to its starting position. Continue this sidestepping movement for about 10 to 15 feet in one direction, then go back the same way, for the same distance, in the opposite direction.
- Rest for 40 seconds or so, and repeat the back-and-forth one more time.

**SCAN FOR VIDEO**

## Clamshell #6

This will engage your glutes while it strengthens your hips muscles and hip flexors.

---

- Begin by lying down on one side, with a resistance band or tube looped or tied just above your knees. Lie on one side with one leg on top of the other—stacked with your knees bent at a 45-degree angle. Keep your top foot down as you raise your top knee as high as you can, creating tension in the looped band.
- Hold for 5 seconds, then lower your top knee back down. Perform 8 to 10 reps, then roll over to repeat the exercise on the other side.

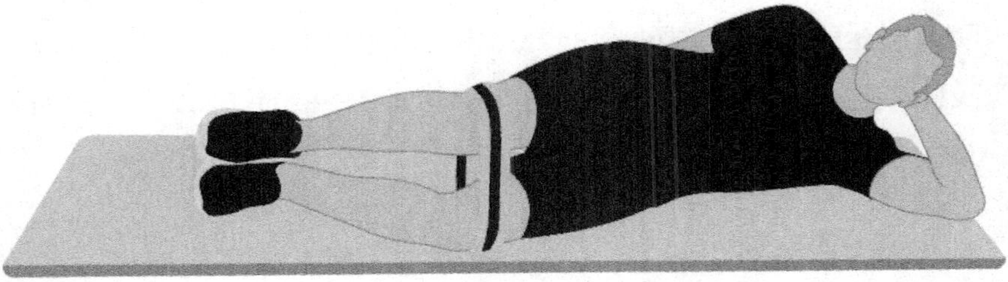

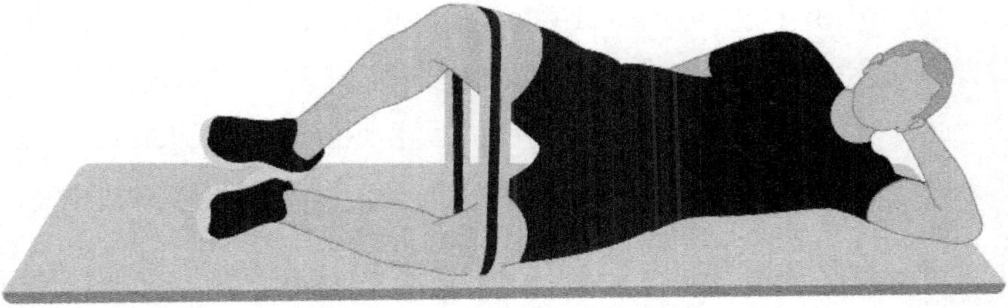

**SCAN FOR VIDEO**

## Side Leg Lift #7

This is similar to the clamshell, but with your legs fully extended. It benefits your hip joints and flexors, and your quadriceps.

---

- Again, lie on your side with an exercise band or tube looped or tied just above your ankles. Place your head on your lower arm as you place your other hand on the floor in front of your chest; this will help you keep your balance. Keep your legs straight with your upper leg on top of the lower leg.
- While keeping your body steady, slowly raise your upper leg as high as you are able, extending the band as you push against its resistance.
- Hold for 5 seconds and lower your upper leg back down. Perform 8 to 10 reps, then roll over to repeat the exercise on the other side.

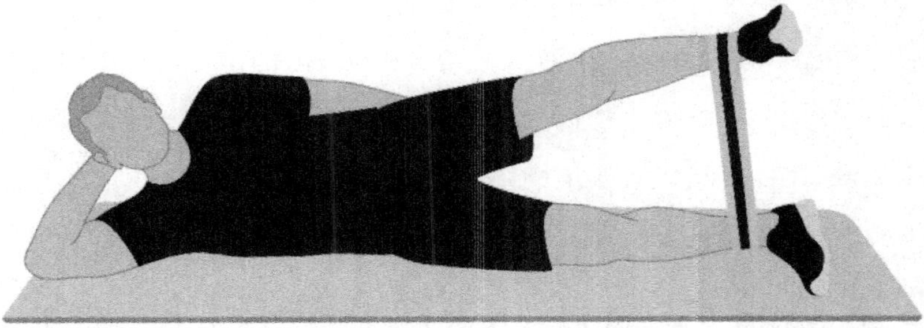

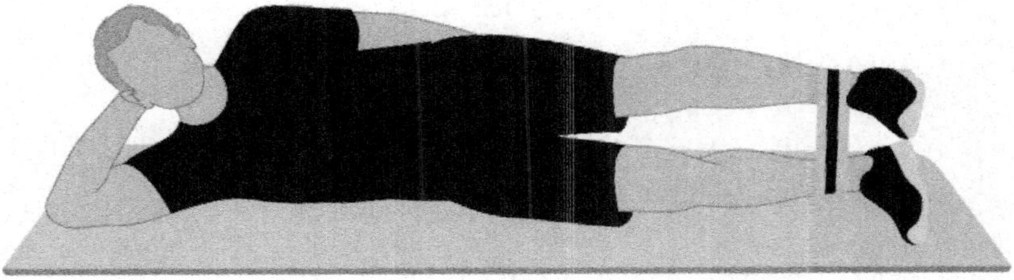

**SCAN FOR VIDEO**

## Chest Press #8

Consider this exercise to be like a standing push up. It will help strengthen your arms, shoulders, and upper back, improving your posture.

---

- Wrap the band around your back and pull it up so it's directly under your armpits. Hold each end of the band with your hands by your armpits and ensure there's no slack in the band.
- Reach out and extend your arms directly in front of you, keeping your hands and the ends of the band at chest level. Extend your arms fully, pause, then slowly return to the starting position, bringing your hands back, close to your body.
- Perform 10 to 12 repetitions, rest for 20 to 30 seconds, then do a second set. If you are able, perform a third set after another brief rest.

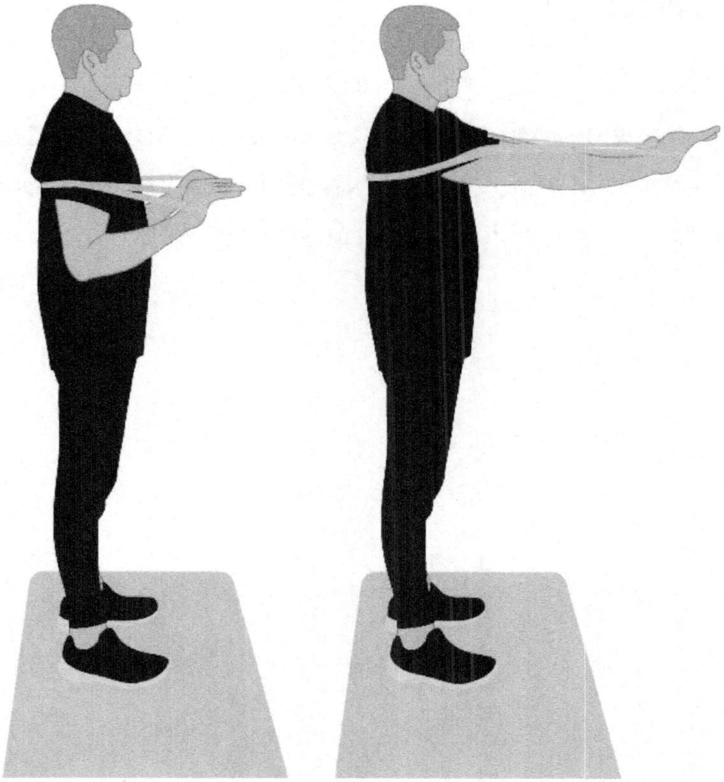

**SCAN FOR VIDEO**

## Onward!

You're now underway, and you've learned some of the best basic starter exercises; now let's advance to more intermediate movements that you can use to focus on your own specific developmental needs.

# CHAPTER 5

# Intermediate Resistance Band Exercises

*It's going to be a journey. It's not a sprint to get in shape.*

Kerri Walsh Jennings
three-time Olympic gold medalist
volleyball champion

## Moving up and Getting Stronger

With the basic resistance band exercises under your belt, it's time to move up a notch to learn a range of intermediate level movements. These exercises are more challenging than the basics, so practice them carefully by following the instructions, and go slowly at first, so that you are able to keep good form and correct posture.

Another important consideration for intermediate level resistance training is to be sure to have adequate tension (or resistance) as you perform the movements. What does this mean? You should be able to feel at least some resistance as you begin the movement, and that tension should increase to a level that you really feel during peak effort.

Make sure the effort is not so difficult that you feel a deep strain or any pain. If you do, stop, and lower the resistance level of the band, or reduce the degree or length of the stretch.

Remember the Hippocratic edict "First, do no harm," which becomes more relevant as the intensity of your workouts increase. Don't strain or injure yourself; the goal is to stay healthy and fit enough to keep on a consistent resistance training schedule.

## *Lower Body Intermediates*

### Hip Thrust #9

This variation of the popular hip thrust will further strengthen and improve your hips through improving their connecting muscles' range of motion.

---

- After placing your feet in the end loops and placing the center of the band in your lap, slide your hips down to the floor, and slide your feet forward about two feet from your bottom. Begin the movement by raising your hips up off the floor—as high as you can without straining.
- Hold this position for 5 to 10 seconds, then lower your hips to the floor to complete 1 rep.

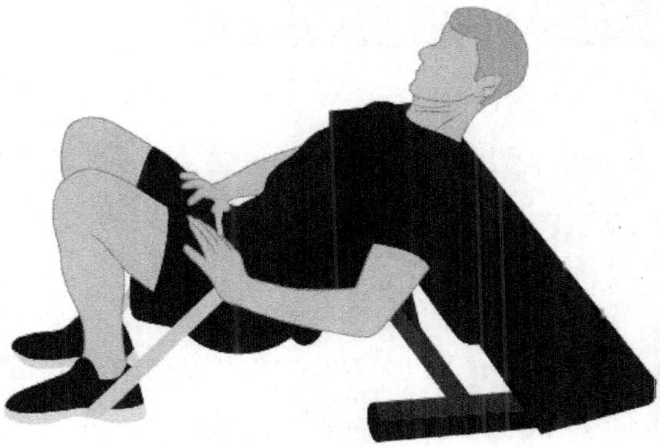

**SCAN FOR VIDEO**

## Bulgarian Split Squat #10

While all squat exercises can benefit the upper thighs, especially the quadriceps, this version adds additional resistance, so the strengthening effect is increased.

---

- Stand with your back to a sturdy chair or sofa. Take a long looped resistance band that can reach from head to toe; if necessary, tie two shorter bands together to create a larger loop.
- Stand on one end of the looped band with your right foot, placed about 18 to 24 inches forward of your left foot. Place the upper end of the loop around the back of your neck. Lift your left foot backward and place it on the chair or sofa.
- *Be careful:* you may want to have a table or counter next to you to hold on to for balance.
- Begin the squat by bending your right knee and lowering your body, being careful to maintain an upright posture—no bending your back! Dip down as far as you can without causing knee pain, pause, then slowly rise back up to complete 1 rep.
- Perform 8 to 12 reps, then lower your left foot to the floor to step forward on the band, placing your right foot behind you on the chair or sofa, and repeating the exercise on the other side by bending your left knee.

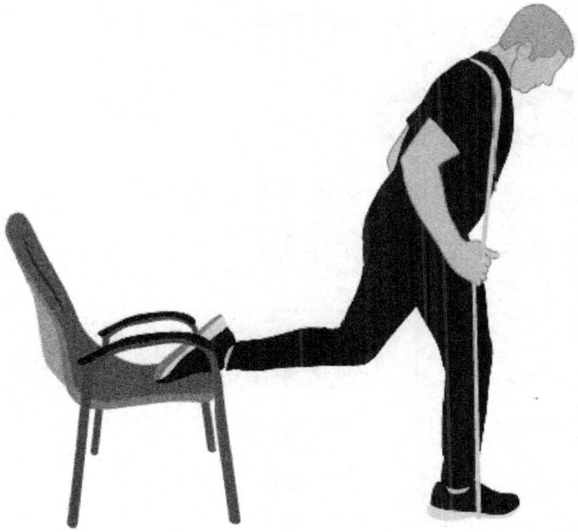

**SCAN FOR VIDEO**

## *Upper Body Intermediates*

### Pull Down #11

Your arms and shoulders will benefit from this exercise, which also strengthens your lats, upper back, and chest.

---

- Use a long looped resistance band (or tie together the ends of a long straight band to form a loop), and fold it in half. Or use a smaller looped band which needs no folding. Insert your hands into the center of the loop, and lightly press your wrists outward, holding the looped band in place.
- Raise your arms up towards the ceiling, keeping the loop open with your wrists pressed lightly outward. Begin the movement by first spreading your arms outward so that they're at a 45-degree angle (or as far as you are able to go without straining).
- Continue the movement by pulling your arms directly downward until your elbows are pointing toward the floor and the band is either close to or touching your chest. Pause for 1 second, then raise your arms back up and release the tension, making sure to maintain light pressure with the wrists to hold the band in place). This completes 1 rep.
- Do a total of 10 to 20 reps, rest for 30 to 40 seconds, then do a second, and if able, a third set.

**SCAN FOR VIDEO**

## Banded Push Up #12

Here's how to use a resistance band or tube to make traditional push-ups more challenging. This movement will strengthen your shoulders, upper arms, upper back, and midbody core muscles.

- Take a resistance band or tube; it can be a single length or a large looped band. Place the band behind your shoulders and place your hands—which are grasping the band—in front of your shoulders. Get down on all fours, slide your feet backwards to straighten your legs, and lay your chest on the floor, with your hands (holding the band) beneath your shoulders. Tighten the band so there's no slack.
- Begin the exercise by pushing up and fully extending your arms. You should feel the resistance of the band, making the upward movement harder than without a band. Slowly lower back down to complete 1 rep.
- Do 10 reps, pause for 30 seconds, then continue to do a second set. Once you are conditioned, you may do a third set, and/or increase the level of resistance of the band you are using, or use two bands.

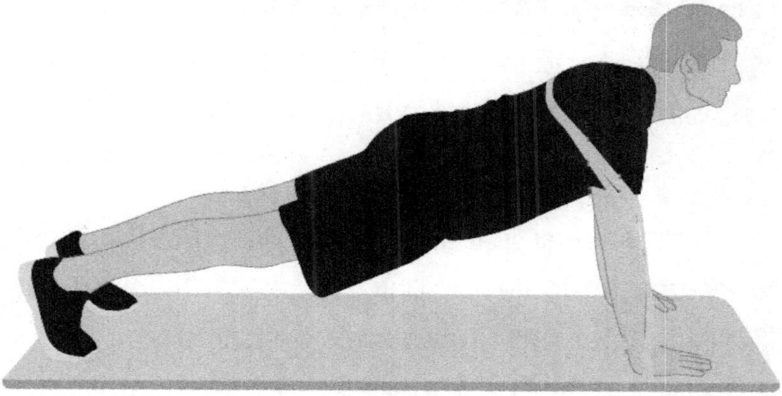

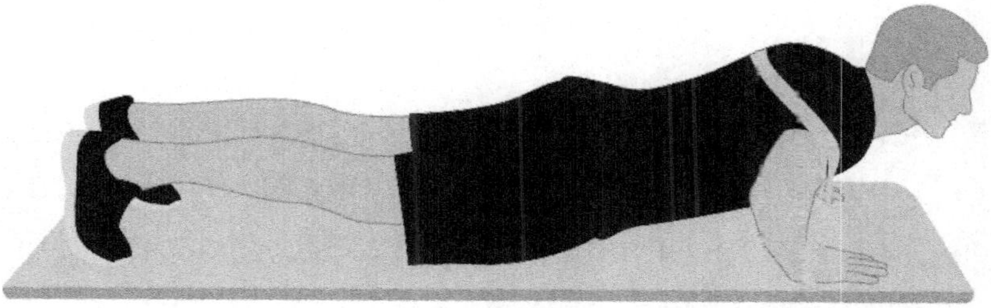

**SCAN FOR VIDEO**

## One Arm Shoulder Press #13

Your shoulders and lats are the primary beneficiaries of this simple but effective movement.

---

- Stand on a large looped band with your right foot, or use a single (or pair) of straight flat bands. Place your right hand into the upper end of the loop or wrap the upper end of the straight band around your right hand. Raise your right hand to your right shoulder.
- Begin the press by pushing your right hand directly upward towards the ceiling, fully extending your arm. Pause for a moment, then slowly lower your right hand back to your right shoulder. Perform 8 to 12 reps, then repeat with your left side. Do two or three sets, with 20 seconds rest between sets.
- You can increase the intensity of the press by tightening the band or using a higher resistance level.

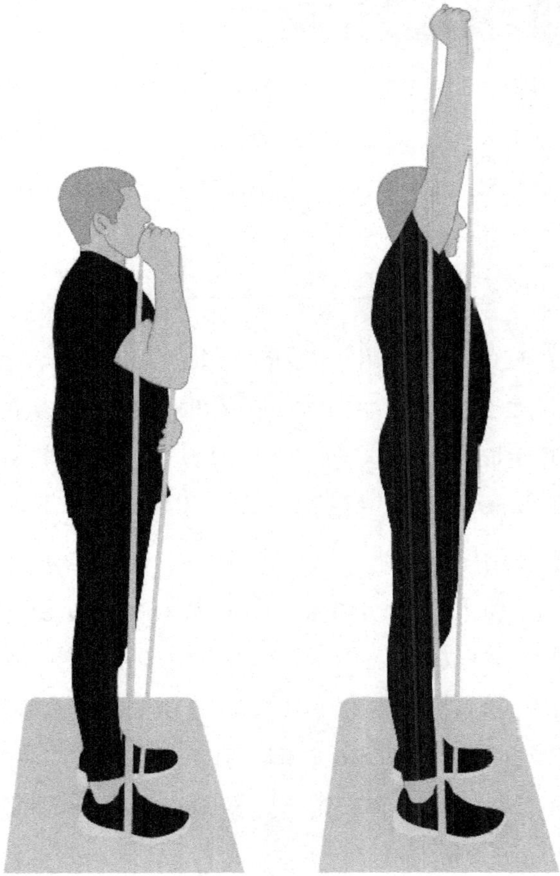

**SCAN FOR VIDEO**

## One Arm Row #14

This is a fundamental shoulder and chest exercise that is typically performed with weights or cable machines; this version uses your resistance bands without the need for weights.

---

- Stand upright with your feet shoulder-width apart, and your left foot about 24 inches forward of your right. Place a looped resistance band or tube under *both feet* to hold the band in place and partially stretch it.
- With your right hand, bend forward at the waist and grasp *both sections* of the looped band at the center, and extend your right arm downward. If the band seems loose and without tension with your arm fully extended, spread your feet to stretch the band slightly.
- Begin the exercise by pulling your right hand straight up, and try to point your right elbow towards the ceiling. Pause when you've gone as far up as you can, then slowly lower your right hand to the starting position.
- Perform 10 to 12 reps, and switch the position so you can repeat the one arm row with your left arm. A second set is recommended after a 20 to 30 second rest.

**SCAN FOR VIDEO**

## *Mid Body Intermediates*

### Bend Over #15

You will both loosen and strengthen your lower back, and the rest of the core muscles which surround your body, including the sides, and front abdominals.

---

- Stand upright and step on a large looped resistance band with both feet. Wrap the upper end of the loop over your head, onto the back of your neck. You should feel a good amount of resistance in this position; if needed, grasp the band and push it out to both sides to increase the stretch.
- Begin the movement by leaning forward from the waist, keeping your back straight, and your knees slightly flexed. Extend forward until your upper body is parallel to the floor, then pause, and slowly rise back up to the erect position. (It is during the upward movement that you should feel the resistance).
- Continue bending up and down for 10 to 15 reps. Rest for 30 seconds, then repeat for a second, and if able, a third set.

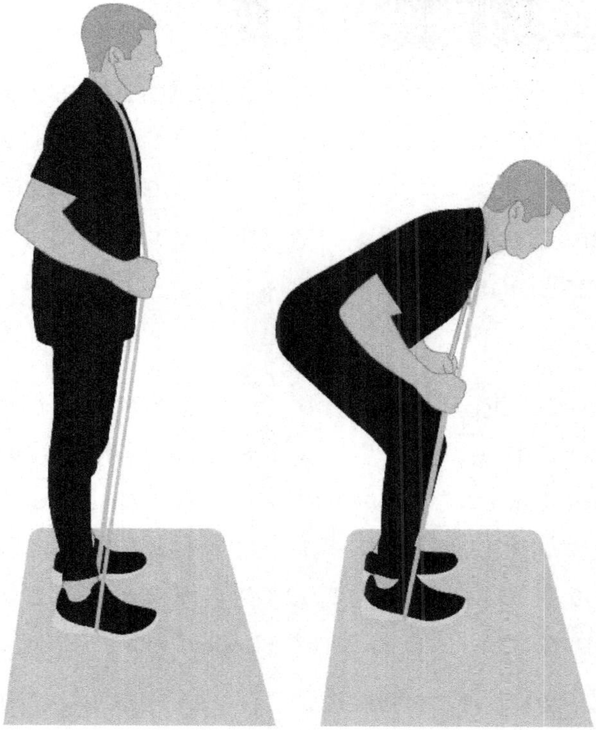

**SCAN FOR VIDEO**

## Banded Dead Bug #16

Your core will be strengthened by this exercise, which is performed lying on a yoga mat or carpet to protect your back. Using your legs to extend the band will also help stretch and strengthen your legs, especially the hamstrings.

---

- Use a loop mini-band, or tie a straight band into a loop about 12 to 18 inches long. While lying on your back, loop the band over your right foot and hold the other end of the band in your right hand. For the starting position, raise both knees and point them upward, while extending your right hand upward.
- Begin the movement by extending your right leg forward, and pulling back on the band with your right hand; you can adjust the level of band resistance by the degree that you pull back. Return your right leg and right arm to the starting position to complete 1 rep. (in the video clip a very strong band is being used, therefore the arm didn't pull back however, as you can see the arm muscles were still fully engaged to maintain it's position, this is perfectly fine)
- Do about 12 reps on the right side, then switch and do 12 on the left side. Be sure not to go too fast, and to maintain a good amount of tension on the band for resistance.

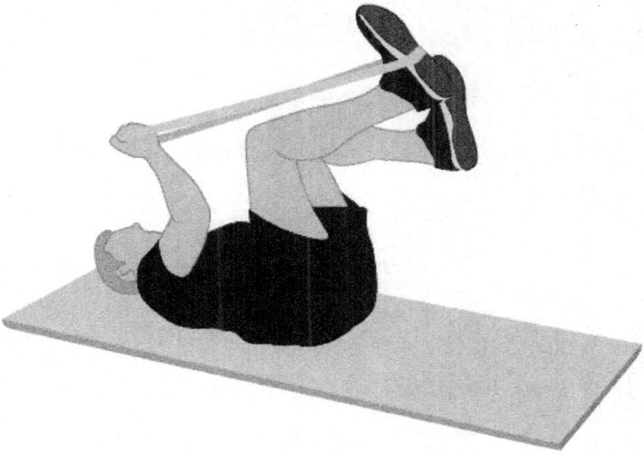

**SCAN FOR VIDEO**

## Banded Plank Walk #17

The upper and lower abdominals and the entire core will gain strength and endurance from the exercise, and it will also be of benefit to your legs and shoulders.

---

- Place a mini loop band around your legs, just above your knees. Assume the push up or straight arm plank starting position with both arms fully extended, your back straight, and your lower body supported on your toes.
- Begin by pulling your right knee forward towards your chest and placing your right foot on the floor. Now pull your left leg forward in the same manner, so both knees are now in the same forward position. Continue by first returning your right leg to the starting, fully extended position, then follow with the left leg. You should now be back to the original plank position.
- Repeat the right-then-left movements for 8 to 10 reps, pause for 30 seconds, then do a second set.

**SCAN FOR VIDEO**

## *Special Exercises*

Before moving forward to Advanced exercises, we're going to cover special exercises for when you are recovering from injury, and when circumstances require you to perform movements while seated.

CHAPTER 6

# Resistance Training for Special Conditions

*I just knew if it could be done, it had to be done, and I did it.*

Gertrude Ederle
Olympic swimming champion;
world record holder

## Injury Recovery and Seated Workouts

This group of specialized resistance exercises is for when you are recovering from injury, or if you can't comfortably perform resistance training while standing; alternatives that are done while you are seated, and which offer the same benefits of strengthening and muscle development as their standing versions.

Seated resistance exercises are not limited to those who have difficulty standing, or with keeping their balance. Anyone can use these seated movements to perform a full body workout, or to focus on specific muscle groups, for example the upper body, core, and lower body.

## *Recovery Band Exercises for Injuries*

No matter how much you think that injuries are what happen to other people, a day may come when you get hurt during a workout or develop an injury through an accumulation of small injuries from many workouts. It may be a slight strain that will go away in a matter of days, or more often, it can be a more serious tear or pull that will take some time and attention in order to fully heal.

## Immediate Action

If you feel pain from a pull, strain, or other exercise-induced discomfort, there is a set of actions abbreviated as 'RICE', which stands for Rest, Ice, Compression, and Elevation.

- Whether this is effective is under debate among doctors and trainers, but it's worth trying. Whenever I suffer any minor pulls or strains, I've found the RICE method to reduce the symptoms, especially if applied immediately after the problem occurs.
- Apply ice wrapped in a protective cloth as soon as possible after the injury to help reduce swelling; similarly, elevation may limit swelling if this is done soon after the injury has been sustained.
- Be careful that any compression does not aggravate the injury, especially if there is any risk of a broken bone.

## Get It Checked

Any injury that lasts more than a few days needs medical attention, so if you're hurting, head to the doctor and get it checked out. X-rays or a scan may be necessary to get an inside look at what's going on, and the prognosis may require treatment.

If the injury isn't too serious, there's a good chance you can manage the recovery through healing practices such as outlined by a professional, and some rest. Below, you'll find tips on the basics of what to do and when to do it in order to minimize trauma, and get you back to working out as quickly as possible.

You might think that rest is the only way to treat injuries, but it's actually a combination of rest plus light exercise that often works best. The key is to select exercises that encourage flexibility without straining or aggravating the injury. Bands can be safely used at low resistance levels, and given their portability, can be carried most anywhere, and used when needed.

According to *GND Fitness* (2022), resistance bands can support recovery from "Tennis elbow, IT band injury, ankle sprain, knee strain, dislocated shoulder, and hip bursitis." As noted earlier, resistance bands can strengthen weak, porous bones to prevent the progression of osteoporosis, and reduce the risks of broken bones.

## Go Lighter in Resistance

Recovery requires a reversal of the training to build and strengthen muscles; instead of doing, say, 8 to 12 reps in a set, to recover safely you should be able to perform 20 or even 30 reps. And even then, you should stop as soon as it starts to become difficult, resisting the temptation to push on.

Assuming you'll be using very light resistance, you can perform many of the resistance band exercises we've already covered in previous chapters, especially those introduced in the chapter for beginners, such as:

- Chest pull aparts, seated rows, lat pull downs, leg extensions, pallof press, side leg lifts, clamshells, and banded side-steps.
- You may also try some of the intermediate exercises, as long as you are careful to keep the resistance at the lowest levels possible.

"Be patient, make gradual improvement and let your body guide you to full recovery and you will soon be back to your pre-injury condition," *GND Fitness* (2022) counsels.

## Seated Resistance Band Exercises

***Take a seat, literally.*** For the following exercises, you'll simply need a regular chair that is sturdy, and not likely to tip over easily. The chair should be without arms, which may constrain your movements or range of motion.

Alternatively, you can sit on a bench, whether it's in a fitness center, a park, or your office. You can be seated anywhere you'd like to do these convenient and safe resistance band workouts:

- Why be seated? As we mature, our balance can diminish, and certain standing movements may become harder to do without the risk of falling.

- Some seniors experience difficulty standing or walking, may be in a wheelchair, or need a walker or rollator to get around. For those with any of these challenges, being able to have a complete resistance training workout while seated is an extremely valuable option.

Even if you are fully mobile, doing your workout while seated can provide a variation in your routine, and maybe work some muscle groups differently. So, I invite you to give the following a try, with the pleasant discovery that they're as beneficial as fitness experts say they are.

## Pointed Toes #18

This fairly simple yet effective movement, performed one leg at a time, will work your lower leg muscles, calves, ankles, and feet.

---

- Sit upright and face forward, holding one end of a long resistance band or tube in each hand. Place your right foot on the center of the band so it's up against the ball of your foot. Pull the band to create tension as you extend your right leg fully outward and up to hip height, or as high as you can.
- Flex your foot by tilting your toes back towards your knee, pausing, then bending your foot in the opposite direction, forward then downward. Return your foot to the starting position to complete 1 rep. Be sure there is tension throughout the entire movement.
- Do 5 slow, deliberate reps with the right foot, and 5 with the left. Pause, then do a second set of 5 reps with each foot.

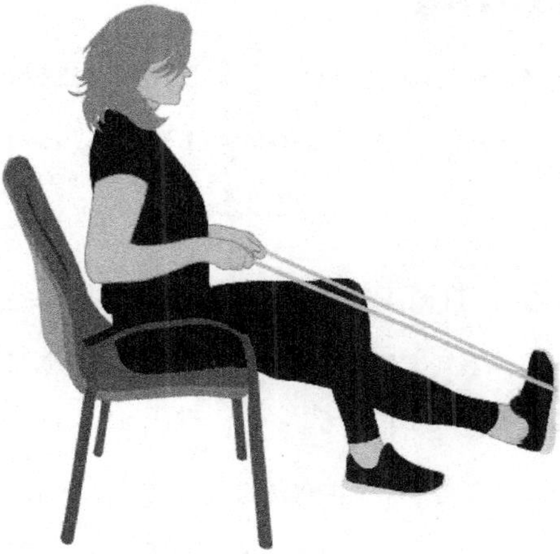

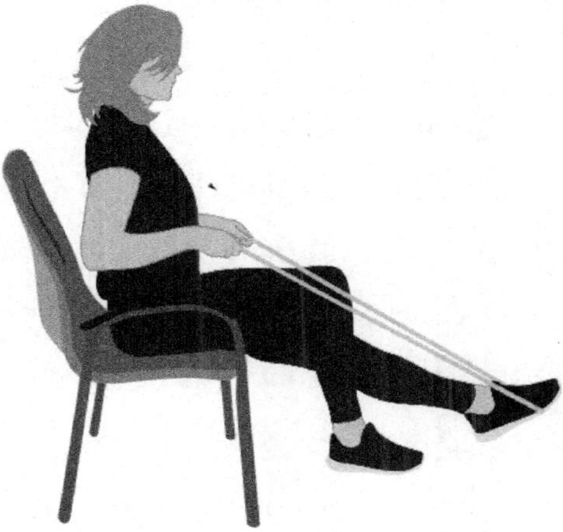

**SCAN FOR VIDEO**

## Leg Lift #19

Your quadriceps—the strong, large muscles in the front of your thighs—are the primary beneficiary of this move.

---

- Begin as in the previous exercise, seated upright, with one foot on the center of the band so it's up against the ball of your foot, while holding the ends of the band in each hand. Fully extend your leg, taking up any slack, and pull on the band to create tension.
- Slowly raise your leg so your toes are pointing toward the ceiling; take it up to hip-level or as close as you can, being sure to keep the band tense so your leg has to work hard. Hold your leg up for 5 to 10 seconds.
- Lower your leg to the starting position, pause for a second or two, then repeat for a total of 5 reps. Switch, and do the same with the other leg. You may do a second, and possibly a third set if you are up to it.

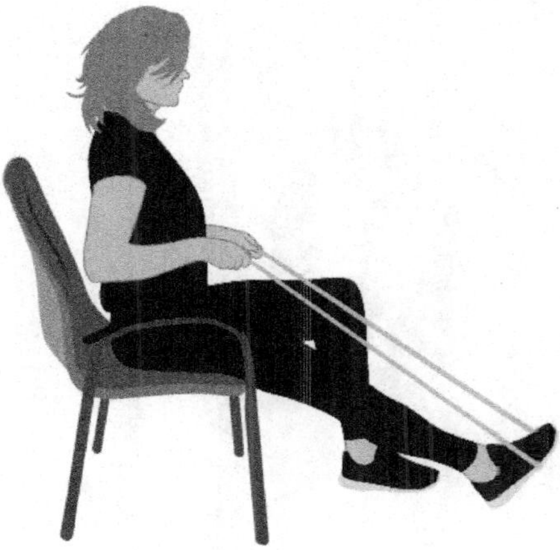

**SCAN FOR VIDEO**

## Modified Leg Lift

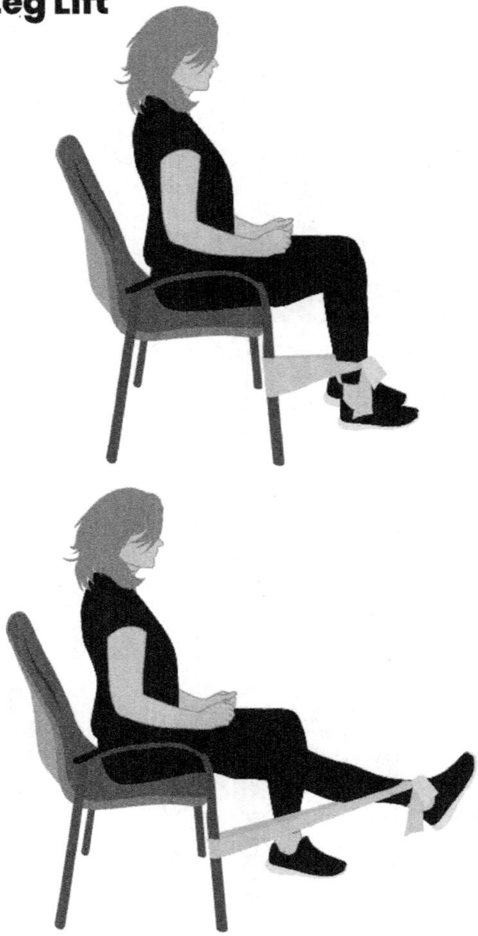

**SCAN FOR VIDEO**

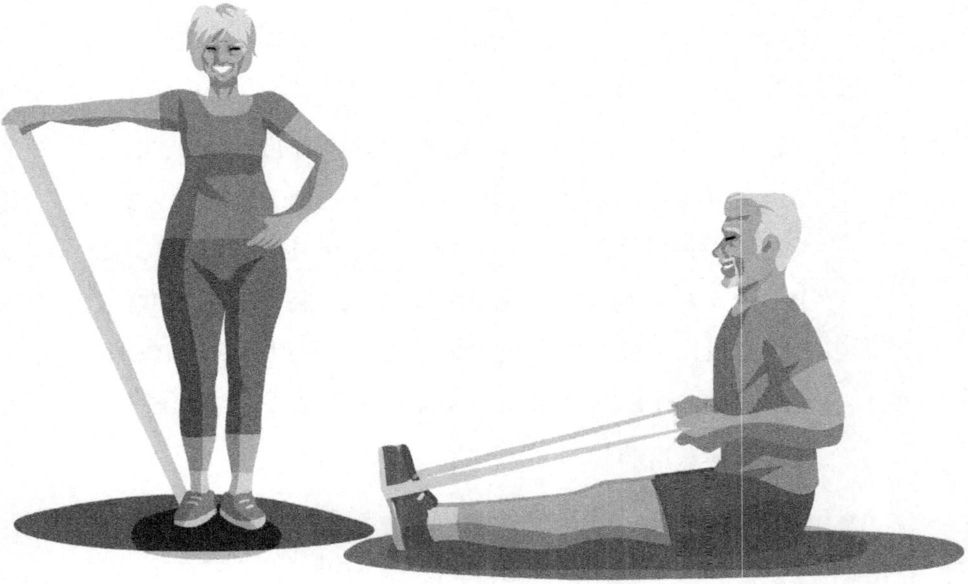

## Leg Press #20

This third leg exercise benefits the quads, hamstrings, glutes, and hips.

---

- This also begins in the same position as the previous two exercises; you should be seated upright with the band against the ball of the foot, with your leg extended and raised.
- Holding the band with each hand, pull as you bend the knee of the raised leg, pulling it back towards your chest. Continue pulling on the resistance band as you then extend your leg back to its starting position. You should feel a good amount of tension as your leg straightens and your foot moves forward.
- Do a total of 5 to 10 reps with each leg, pausing for 20 to 30 seconds before performing a second set. Depending on how much resistance is involved, you may be able to do a third set.

**SCAN FOR VIDEO**

## Hip Opening #21

This is the last of the moderate level leg exercises; it tenses and strengthens the muscles of the hip joints and thighs, with the secondary benefit of strengthening the glutes.

---

- While seated, take a long resistance band and lay it across your thighs, just behind your knees. Now wrap the band around your thighs by folding each end under your thighs and pulling the ends directly upward. You should have now formed a loop that extends completely around your thighs. Maintain tension by holding the bands upward.
- Lift your right foot slightly, and swing your right leg out to the side, increasing the resistance and feeling the tension in your right thigh and hip. Hold for 2 or 3 seconds before returning to the center position.
- Do a total of 5 to 8 reps, then repeat with your left leg. You may do additional sets if able.

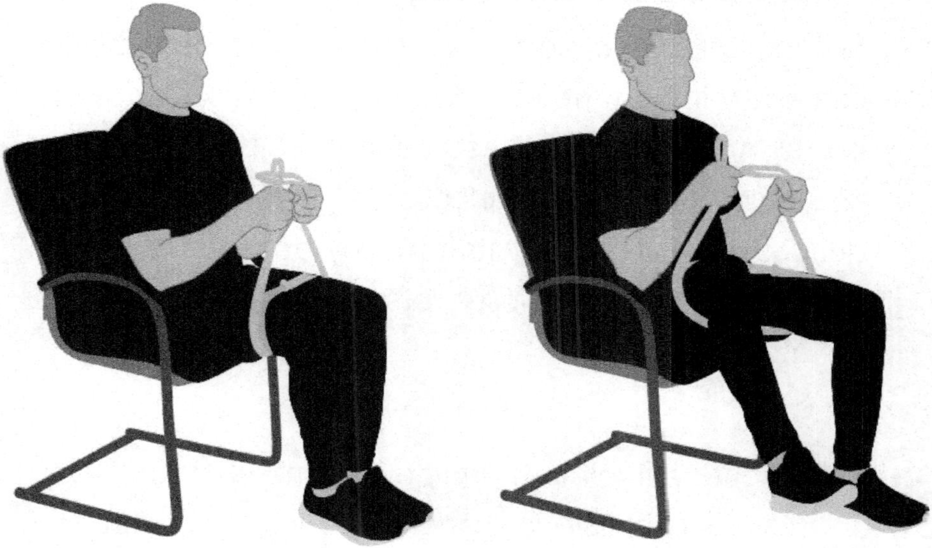

**SCAN FOR VIDEO**

## Abdominal Lean #22

Moving on to our core, the abdominal muscles are extremely important; they support our trunk, allow for better movement and less chance of back injuries, and hold our organs in place. The following move is deceptively simple, but its efficacy depends on your keeping tension on the resistance band throughout the movement.

---

- Seat yourself in the middle of the chair to leave space behind you, and place your feet flat on the floor, about hip-distance apart. Hold the resistance band or tube at shoulder level, stretched sufficiently to create a good amount of tension.
- Sit up straight, keeping your head, neck, and spine in vertical alignment; tighten your abdominals to engage your core.
- Begin the exercise by leaning as far back as you can to feel tension in the abdominals. Hold for 5 seconds, then rise back up to the upright position to complete 1 rep.
- Perform 10 reps, being careful to go back and forward slowly to fully benefit from the exercise. Rest for 20 seconds, then do a second set.

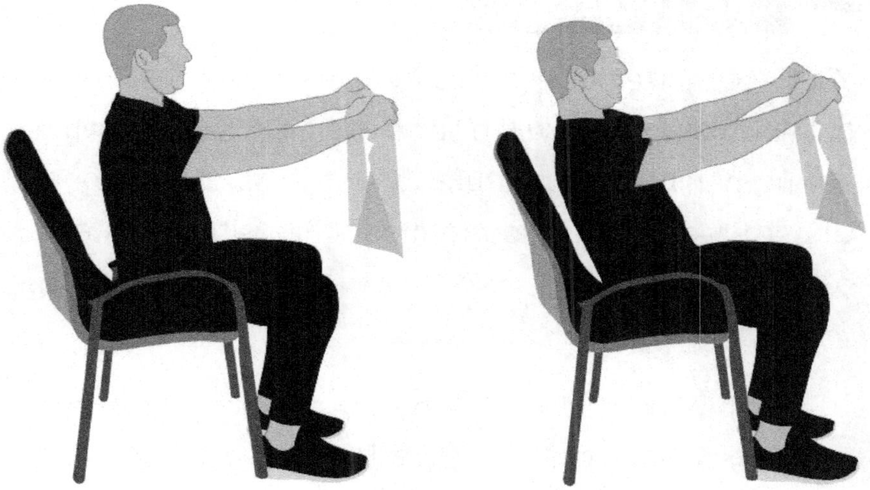

**SCAN FOR VIDEO**

## Chest Press #23

You'll recognize this exercise from the previous chapter, but now you'll see how the same exercise, with the same strengthening and postural benefits as a traditional Chest Press, can be performed while sitting instead of standing.

---

- While seated in an upright position, wrap the resistance band or tube behind your back and place it just below your armpits. Hold each end of the band and pull enough to ensure there's no slack in the band.
- Extend your arms forward at chest height. Pause when your arms are fully straightened, then slowly return them to the starting position, bringing your hands close to your body.
- Perform 10 to 12 reps; the resistance level should be enough for these reps to be challenging. Rest for 20 to 30 seconds, then do a second set. If you are able, a third set can follow another brief rest period.

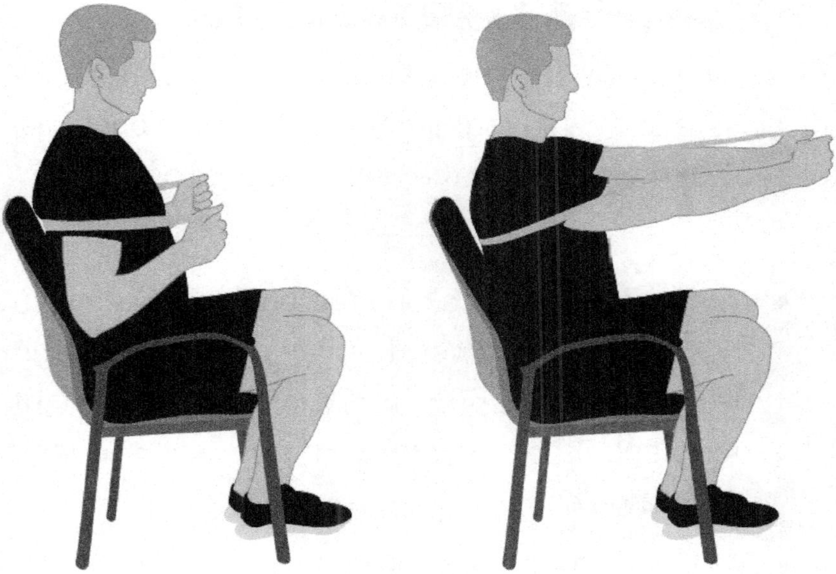

**SCAN FOR VIDEO**

## Shoulder Press (Upwards) #24

This exercise will isolate the shoulder's rotator cuff muscles, and also strengthen the muscles of your arms, especially the triceps in the rear of your upper arms.

---

- While seated, hold a long resistance band in your right hand, and lower the other end of the band to the floor. Step on the band with your right foot, and reach up with your right hand to your right shoulder.
- At this point, there should be light tension in the band; if it's not tense enough, shorten the length between your hand and foot, and if it's too tense, lift your right foot and release some slack.
- Begin the exercise by lifting your right hand directly upward, pressing it towards the ceiling, and extend until your arm is straight. (Be sure to keep your right foot firmly in the band—don't let it slip out).
- Pause for 2 seconds, then slowly lower your hand back to the starting position. Repeat 10 to 12 times, then switch sides.

**SCAN FOR VIDEO**

## Triceps Extension (v.1) #25

If the previous exercise works your triceps, this one will do so even more. It will also help strengthen your shoulders and wrists.

---

- Be seated, and hold one end of a long resistance band in your right hand, and rest the other end on the floor. Step on that end with your right foot to hold it in place.
- Starting with your right hand by your right hip, pull your right hand up to your shoulder with your elbow pointing to the rear, and make sure there is a moderate amount of tension—not too much.
- Continue the movement by straightening your right arm as you swing it back, so your right hand is now pointing to the rear. Be sure to fully extend your right arm. Pause, then rotate your right hand to return it to your shoulder, and point your right elbow to the rear. This completes 1 rep.
- Do a total of 8 to 10 reps, then switch to the left side and repeat. Do a second and third set if you are able.

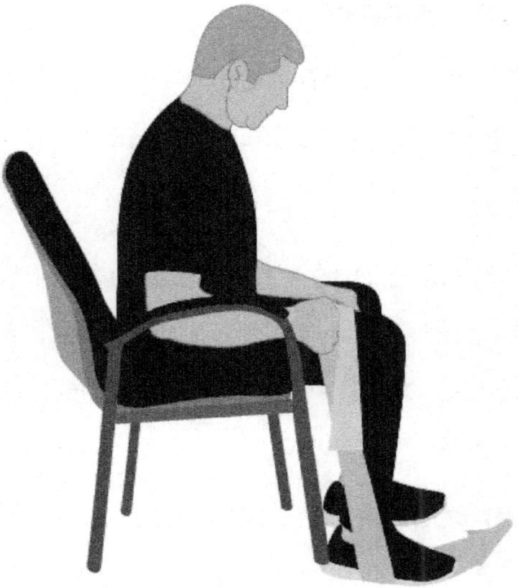

**SCAN FOR VIDEO**

## Triceps Extension (v.2) #26

If the previous triceps press seems complicated, here is a simpler alternative with equally effective results.

---

- Be seated, and as in v.1, hold one end of a long resistance band in your right hand, and rest the other end on the floor. Step on that end with your right foot to hold it in place.
- Raise your right hand to your right shoulder, and ensure there is resistance in the band at this stage. Raise your upper arm until it is parallel to the floor; your elbow is pointing forward, and your right hand is pointing rearward. You should already feel some tightness in your triceps.
- Begin the movement by pulling the band upward and forward at about a 45-degree angle. Pause for 2 to 3 seconds, then return your hand and arm to the starting position. This completes 1 rep.
- Perform 8 to 10 reps, then switch to the left side and repeat. Do a second and third set if you are able.

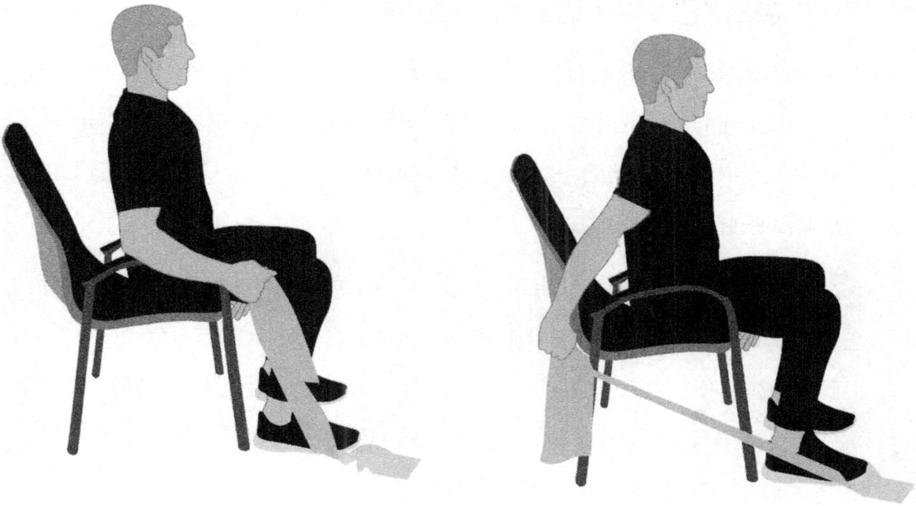

**SCAN FOR VIDEO**

## Biceps Curl (v.1) #27

This classic is often performed by weightlifters in a seated position on a bench with a backrest; you can do the same in a chair using your resistance bands, and with equal benefits.

While seated, hold the band in your right hand, and step on the other end with your right foot. To achieve the correct resistance, hold your arm fully extended downward, with your hand at the level of your hip; the band should be without any slack.

Begin by curling your right hand upward, keeping your elbow tight to your side, and raise your hand until it is close to your right shoulder. Pause, then curl your arm and hand downward to the starting position to complete 1 rep.

Do 10 reps, then switch to the left side. Ideally, you should perform a total of three sets; it's okay with this move if you find it hard to do the full number of reps by the third set.

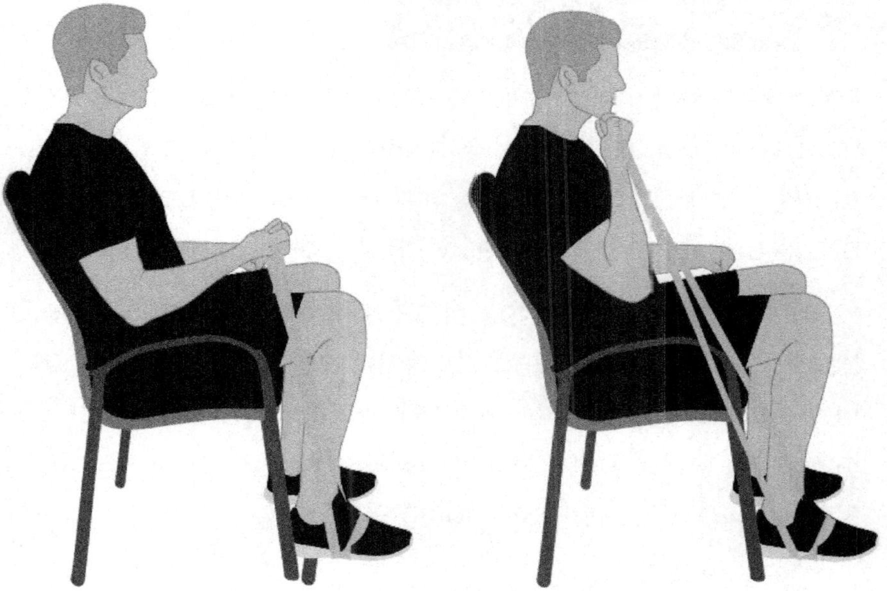

**SCAN FOR VIDEO**

## Biceps Curl (v.2) #28

You can save time by curling with both arms at the same time. This can be done with two resistance bands or tubes, except in this version, you would set up both arms, but in the same manner as with the one-arm option.

Or you can use one long band: Hold each end of the band in each hand, and slide the center of the band beneath both of your feet. As above, eliminate any slack in the band so there's slight tension when your hands are at your hips, before curling upward.

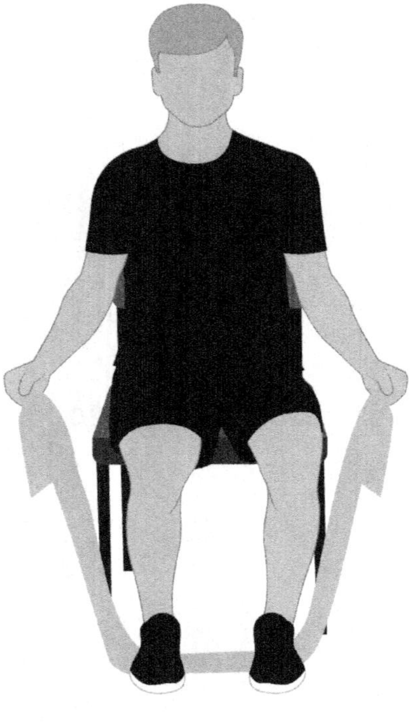

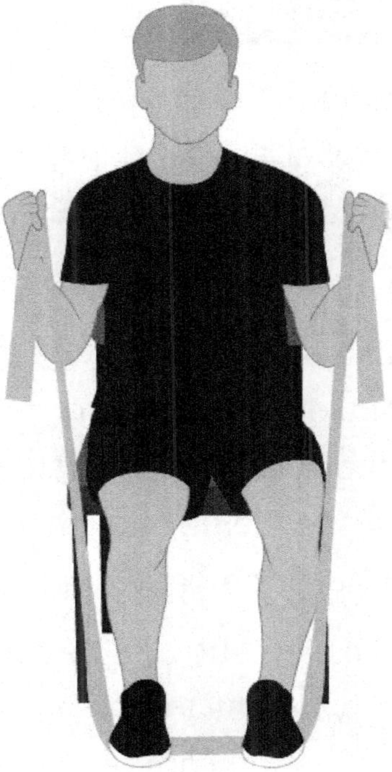

**SCAN FOR VIDEO**

## Chest Stretch #29

You will build strength and endurance in your pectorals (chest muscles), as well as your shoulders and upper arms with this simple yet effective seated upper body exercise.

---

- Hold a resistance band or tube with both hands, spaced shoulder-width apart, extended straight ahead, at shoulder height. Be sure there's no slack in the band, and there's enough resistance to make you work to pull the band apart.
- Begin the movement by stretching the band to both sides, while at the same time pulling your elbows back so they are pointing to the rear. Pull your elbows back until the band reaches your chest (or close to it). Be sure that you are keeping the band stretched apart.
- Slowly return your arms and hands to the starting position to complete 1 rep. Continue until you reach 10 reps, then pause for 20 to 30 seconds, and repeat for one or two more sets.

**SCAN FOR VIDEO**

**Advancing:** Now onto the more challenging set of resistance band exercises, when your strength and balance are ready.

# CHAPTER 7

# Advanced Resistance Band Exercises

*If something stands between you and your success, move it. Never be denied.*

Dwayne 'The Rock' Johnson

## Stepping up to the Challenge

If you feel ready, this is where you can become familiar with the more advanced resistance band exercises. The assumption is that, at this point in your exercise journey, you now feel comfortable with the beginner and intermediate level movements, and are able to perform two to three sets of those exercises with at least a medium level of resistance.

## *A Few Cautions*

**Be careful:** As is customary, it's a good practice to heed a few words of caution. Don't push yourself to overachieve and end up causing injury or excessive fatigue. Remember, resistance training is a marathon, not a sprint; it requires pacing for the long-term benefits you are working towards. Also, stay attentive to your balance, and use these exercises to improve it, continuing to focus on good form and posture.

**Rest:** This is an important yet often overlooked factor in building muscle, no matter how strong and conditioned you feel. Remember to allow at least one day of rest between resistance workouts so your muscles have the necessary time to recover and rebuild. You can work out every day if you wish, but not with the same muscle groups. The alternative is to do full body resistance workouts no more than three times a week.

The following exercises can be combined to give you a rigorous, 20-minute full body workout. "It includes compound movements that work multiple muscle groups at once; the exercises also challenge your core stability and balance," reports physiologist and sports performance coach D'Annette Stephens, ISSA-CPT, in *Livestrong* (2022).

She recommends using two mini bands, plus one long-looped resistance band at levels of resistance that feel hard, rather than easy, "but not too hard that you can't do the moves with good form." (You may also use flat bands or tubes as noted below).

## ***Eight Advanced Movements***

### Pull To Face #30

Your shoulders and upper back are the principal beneficiaries of this exercise.

---

- Attach one end of a long-looped resistance band to an immovable, sturdy object close to head height. Pick up the opposite end of the band with both hands—palms facing out— with your arms extended in front of you. Step back far enough that there's some tension in the band when your arms are fully extended.
- Bend your knees, and lower your body to a quarter squat with your feet placed hip-width apart. Pull the band back to your forehead, focusing on pulling your shoulder blades together, and making sure your elbows are at shoulder height and pointing outwards to the sides when you reach the peak

of the movement. Slowly return your hands to the starting position by extending your arms fully forward.

- This makes 1 rep; perform 10 to 15 reps for 1 set, rest for 20 to 30 seconds, then repeat a second set, and, if able, a third set.
- *Note: You can use a flat band or a tube if you are able to safely attach the far end to a sturdy object and can get a good grip on the end of the band you'll be pulling, or the handles if the tube has them.*

**SCAN FOR VIDEO**

## Front Squat #31

This move will increase strength primarily in your bum and shoulders, and will also work your thighs, especially the quadriceps.

---

- Stand solidly in the center of the band with your feet placed about shoulder-width apart. Take an end of the band in each of your hands and raise them to shoulder height, with your palms facing up. This is the point of maximum resistance in this exercise, so be sure you're feeling a good amount of tension here.
- Keep your back straight and brace (tighten) your core, then force your hips back and bend your knees, to lower your hips until your thighs are parallel with the floor, or as low as you can go without hurting your knees. Remember to keep your back straight, to minimize any bending at the waist.
- Slowly stand back up to the upright position to complete 1 rep. Do three sets of 12 to 15 reps, with a 30 to 40 second rest between sets.

**SCAN FOR VIDEO**

## Single Leg Deadlift #32

You will flex and strengthen your hamstring muscles, your glutes in the butt, as well as your shoulders, making this a 'compound exercise', meaning it works both the upper body and lower body at the same time.

---

- Place a looped band under your left foot, and hold the other end in your right hand, at hip level. There should be a good amount of resistance tension in the band, since this will be the farthest point of its stretch; slide your hand down the band to shorten it, if needed.
- Begin the movement by bending over at the waist, and at the same time, raising your right leg up to the rear, and lowering your right hand towards your right foot, letting the band pull your hand downward. Be sure to keep your back straight as you bend—this is very important in order to prevent back injuries. If you can achieve it, your body and right leg should form a straight, horizontal line.
- Hold this position for a moment, then raise your body back to an upright position, lower your right foot to the floor, and raise your right hand to your right hip. Feel the tension as the resistance in the band increases. This constitutes 1 rep.

- Continue for a total of 15 to 20 reps, then switch sides, bending forward, raising your left leg back and up, and lowering your left hand to your left foot. Do 10 to 12 reps. If you're up to it, do a second set on each side, and once you're conditioned, a third set.

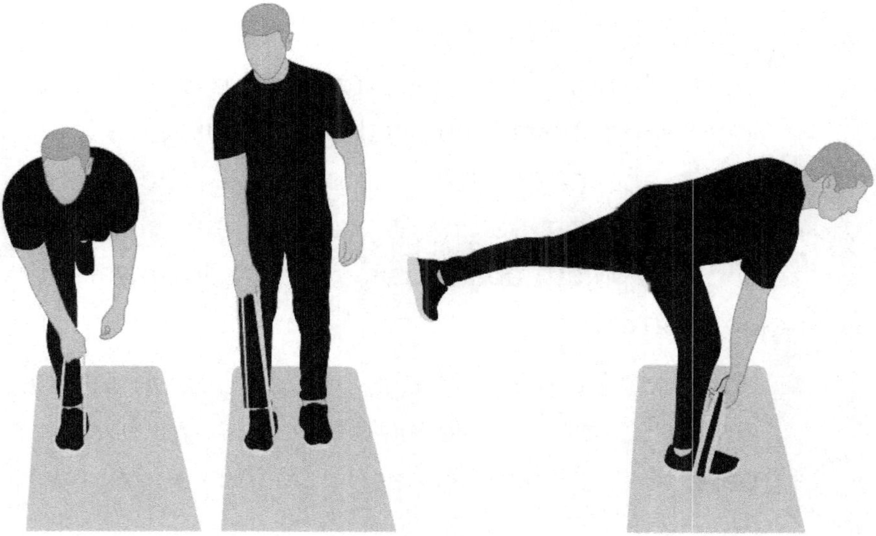

**SCAN FOR VIDEO**

## Clean and Press #33

This is another upper and lower body compound exercise that strengthens the quadricep muscles in your legs, along with other supporting leg muscles, your hip joints, the glutes in your bum, and your shoulders.

---

- Stand upright with your left foot forward and with the right leg to the rear. Step into a long looped resistance band with your leading left foot, and stand on it. Hold the opposite end of the band at waist-height, with both hands spread shoulder-width apart, palms facing downward in an overhand grip.
- Begin the movement by squatting down into a sitting position, while simultaneously raising the band to your shoulders and pointing your elbows downward. Continue the movement by standing upright to come out of the squat, and as you rise up, press the band upward towards the ceiling, and fully extend your arms.
- Return to the starting position by lowering both your hands and the resistance band back to waist height. This completes 1 rep. Do 10 reps, then switch positions with the right foot forward stepping on the band. Do 10 reps to complete a full set. Do a second set, and when you are conditioned and able, do a third set.

- *Note: If you don't have a long looped band, you can perform this exercise with a long flat band, holding each end of the band in each hand, held shoulder-width apart, ensuring you have enough resistance to make the exercise productive.*

**SCAN FOR VIDEO**

## Bear Crawl #34

Here is yet another compound resistance exercise; this move helps to develop your legs and hips, and especially your core, arms, and shoulders.

---

- You will need two small-to-medium sized looped resistance bands, or you can use flat bands or tubes that are tied to make the loops. Step into one loop with both feet so the band is around your ankles; place both hands inside the other loop so it is around your wrists. On a mat or carpet, go down on all fours, with your hands beneath your shoulders, arms fully extended. Raise your knees off the floor so your lower body is supported by your toes. There should be little or no slack in the looped bands to ensure at least a moderate amount of resistance during each movement.
- Begin the exercise by proceeding sideways, advancing your right hand and right foot about six inches (more or less) to the right, then catching up with your left hand and left foot. Immediately continue the movement with the right hand and foot, followed by the left hand and foot. If space permits, take about 10 right advances and left catch-ups.

- Then, reverse the movement so you're now moving to the left, leading with your left hand and foot, and catching up the right hand and foot. Return to the original starting point to complete 1 rep.
- You may be fatigued after one complete set of 10 reps, but if you are able, do a second set after resting for about 20 seconds. A third set can be done when your training has prepared you for it and you can get through it—even with fewer reps, if that's all you can do.
- *Note: If you find this exercise too difficult initially, perform it with only the band around your wrists. You then have the option of taking the 10 steps in each direction, or simply extending your right hand to the side, then returning it to beneath your shoulder, then repeating the same movement with your left hand.*

**SCAN FOR VIDEO**

## Chest Crossover #35

This is a classic movement that is traditionally performed with weights (lying on a bench) or cables; you can do it with equal effectiveness with resistance bands or tubes in a standing position. Your chest's pectoral muscles, commonly referred to as 'pecs' and your latissimus dorsi muscles, referred to as 'lats', which extend from your upper back to your sides, will be the primary beneficiaries, along with your shoulders.

---

- Connect two medium length bands or tubes to a stationary post, or wrap one long band or tube around the post. To assume the starting position, stand with your back to the post and hold each end of the band (or handles of the tube), and raise your arms out to the sides, parallel to the floor at shoulder height. Step forward if needed to create some tension in the band. Your arms should be extended with a slight bend at the elbows, with your palms facing forward.
- Begin the movement by bringing your arms across your chest, keeping your arms straight as your hands form an arc as you bring them together, pointing outward in front of you. Flex your pecs and

hold them contracted as you maintain the position for 2 or 3 seconds, then slowly return your arms to the starting position, keeping them extended throughout the movement. This constitutes 1 rep.

- Repeat, slowly and deliberately, for 10 reps, then relax, wait 30 seconds, then do a second set, and, if you're up to it, a third. If necessary, you can do fewer reps in the later sets, as long as you can do so without compromising your form and upright posture.

**SCAN FOR VIDEO**

## Resistance Crunch #36

The crunch has replaced the sit-up as the favorite abdominals builder; it's the most popular move done by most people who want defined, flat abs, without risking the back strain that sit-ups often cause. But over time, 12 or so reps of crunches can become too easy. That's where weighted crunches come in useful, and you can achieve the same positive results with resistance bands.

There are at least two ways to achieve the needed resistance to intensify your crunches:

---

- **The first way:** Lie on a bench with your head flat and your knees partially raised. Place a resistance band or tube under the bench, below where your head and shoulders are resting. Hold the resistance band in each hand and pull your hands up to the sides of your head, being sure there is some resistance before beginning the movement.
- Start by raising your head, shoulders, and upper back off the bench to perform a crunch, with your head and shoulders only rising about 10 to 12 inches, unlike the sit-up, which takes your elbows all the way to your knees. As you rise upward, if you feel pain in your back, stop, and place a small,

folded towel under your lower back for support then continue.

- Hold the crunch position for at least 3 seconds, tightening your core muscles, then slowly lower your head and shoulders to the bench to complete 1 rep.
- **A second method:** Add resistance by lying on a mat or carpet, with the resistance band attached securely to a post or the leg of a heavy table or dresser, positioned just beyond your head. As described above, hold the resistance band in each hand, and pull your hands up to the sides of your head, being sure there is some resistance before beginning the movement.
- Perform the crunch, feeling the resistance as you rise upward and away from the post or table leg. Be sure to tighten your core, and lower back down slowly.
- Regardless of which method you prefer, perform 12 reps, rest for 20 to 30 seconds, then repeat for a second, and possibly a third set.
- *Note: You may need to adjust the tension in the band so that about 12 crunches are just enough to wear you out.*

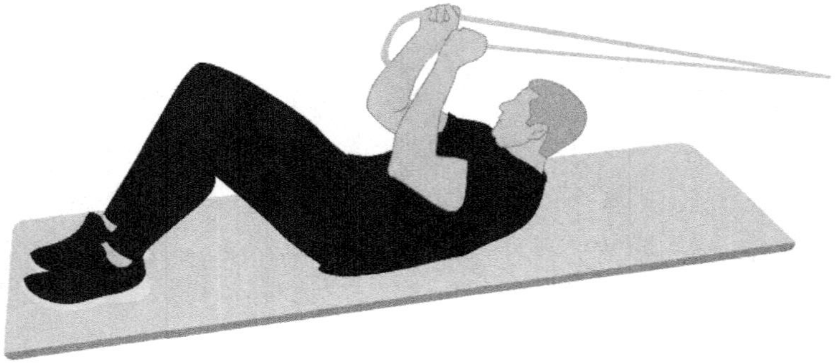

**SCAN FOR VIDEO**

## Lateral Raise #37

This is a simple but highly effective exercise for your shoulders, and secondarily for your arms, wrists, and upper back muscles. It's a standard move, whether done with weights or resistance bands and tubes.

---

- Stand upright with your legs and feet close together (or slightly apart, if needed for balance). Place the center of a long resistance band or tube under your feet and grasp each end with your right and left hands. Hold your hands at your sides, with arms fully extended downward, and your palms facing backwards.
- Raise both hands up at a 45-degree angle, keeping your arms fully extended throughout the movement. Bring your hands up to shoulder level, or just above.
- Hold for a moment, then slowly lower your arms to the starting position. This is 1 rep. Do 10 to 12 reps, rest for 20 to 30 seconds, and follow with a second set.

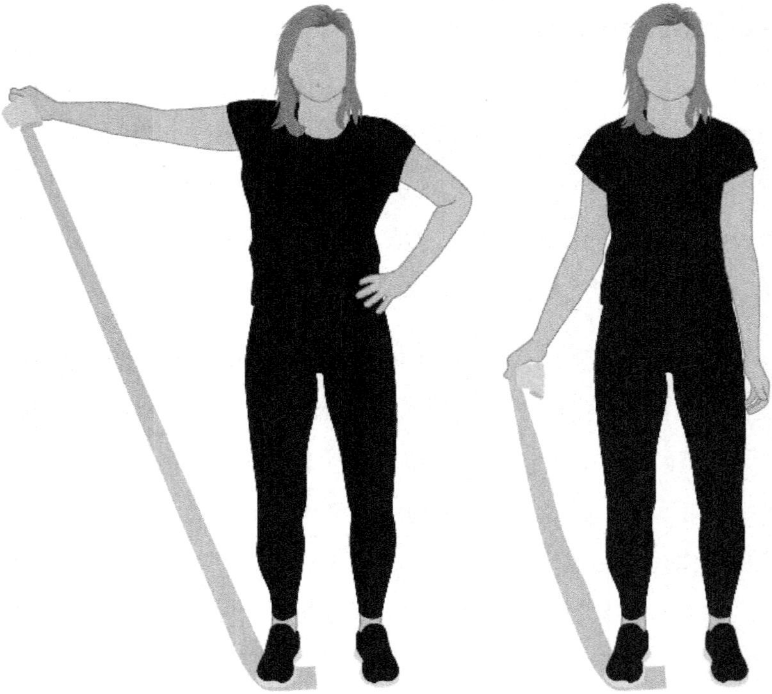

**SCAN FOR VIDEO**

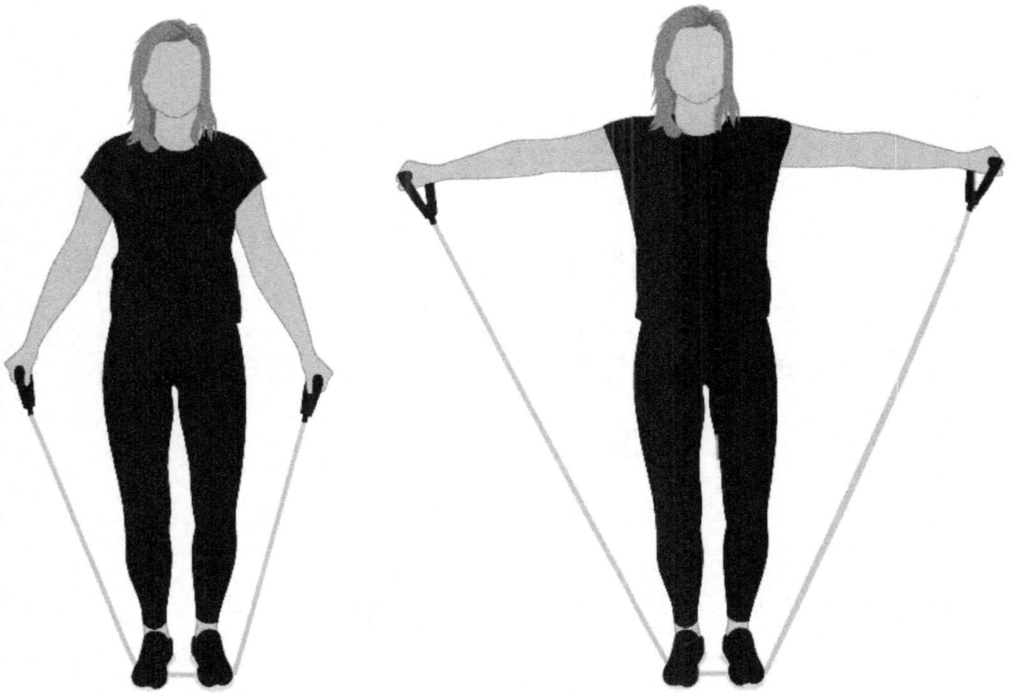

**SCAN FOR VIDEO**

**Next:** You'll learn how your bodyweight can create an extremely effective force of resistance with an increase in intensity when supplemented with resistance bands.

# CHAPTER 8

# Bodyweight Calisthenics and Aerobics

*Champions aren't made in the gyms. Champions are made from something they have deep inside them—a desire, a dream, a vision.*

*Muhammad Ali*

## Getting Even Stronger and Conditioned

You are encouraged to supplement your resistance band training with bodyweight calisthenics and aerobics; two other important forms of exercise that will increase your overall level of physical fitness, make you stronger, and increase your cardiovascular conditioning.

This is not to suggest that a full resistance band exercise program cannot make you as strong as calisthenics, nor does it imply that you can't intensify your resistance band workouts to achieve aerobic conditioning. It's important to note here that it is definitely possible to 'max out' your workouts with continual, vigorous rounds of reps and sets with resistance bands and tubes as your only form of exercise.

Variation in your workouts can help prevent boredom, reduce the risk of injury, and potentially increase your frequency and consistency of working out over the long term.

- You may find 20 to 30 minutes of aerobic jogging, fast walking, cycling, or swimming, for example, to be preferable to hustling through your resistance band workout in an effort to keep your heart pumping at the pace you desire, but now that you're in advanced shape, that could easily cause you to perform the movements too fast, forgetting proper form and posture, which is a recipe for injury.
- Adding some calisthenics without resistance bands is a good way to ensure all your muscle groups are being strengthened, while at the same time getting the best of both techniques by doing calisthenics supplemented with the bands, as noted in previous chapters.

## *Bodyweight Calisthenics*

### Push Ups #38

Push-ups build your shoulders, upper arms, chest, upper back, and core, making them one of the most productive resistance exercises.

---

- We all know this one, but for review, a push up is performed by first getting down on your hands and knees, then extending your legs to the rear, so your weight is suspended solely on your hands and toes. Keep your back straight as you bend your elbows to lower your chest towards the floor. Get as low as you are able to before slowly pushing back up to the starting position, with your arms straight; this completes 1 rep.
- Do as many as you can, working up over time to at least 10 to 12 reps. Rest for 30 to 40 seconds, then do a second set. If your shoulders are holding out, rest again, and do a third set. Remember to keep your back straight—no sagging!
- *Note: If you find that 12 reps are too easy, instead of increasing the reps, slow down the upward and downward movements. For example, take 5 or 10 seconds going down, pause for 5 seconds, then slowly rise back up; you'll feel the difference.*

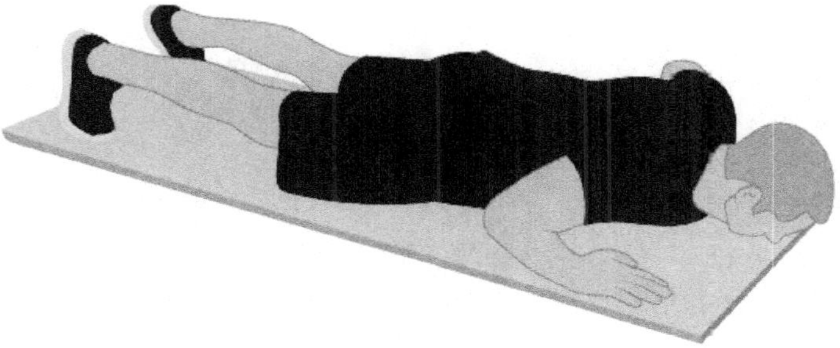

**SCAN FOR VIDEO**

## Modified Push Up

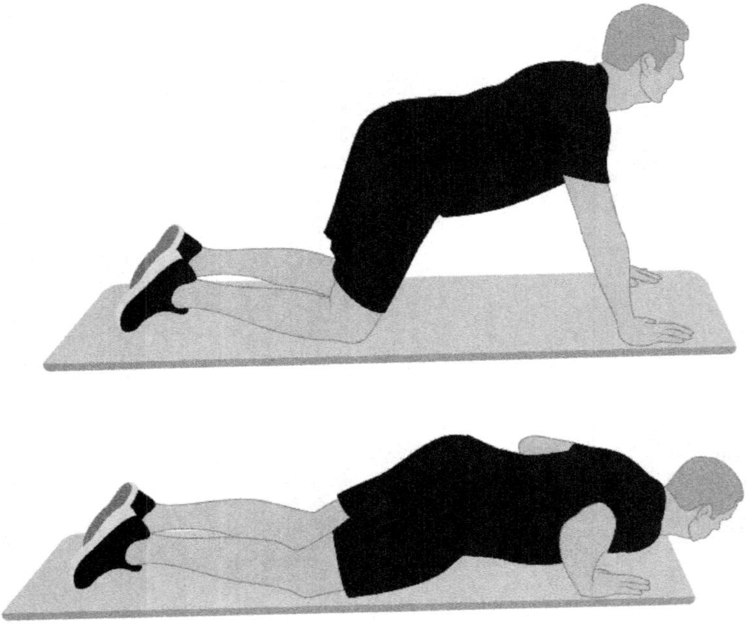

**SCAN FOR VIDEO**

## Planks #39

This close cousin of the push up benefits the same muscle groups, but is a holding exercise, rather than a movement. There are two versions:

---

- **Version 1:** Assume the same starting position as the push up, with arms fully extended. Face downward (not forward) and hold this pose for at least 10 seconds, ideally being able to work up to 30 seconds, or even a full minute, as you become conditioned. Do a second plank after a 30 second rest.
- **Version 2:** The alternative plank pose is to rest your upper body on your forearms, with elbows bent and placed beneath your shoulders. Hold as with the version 1 arms-extended pose, and repeat after a 30 second rest.
- *Note: Be sure to keep your back from sagging or drooping, as this will reduce the benefits to your core. It's imperative with this move that you keep your back straight, all the way up to your shoulders, for it to be effective and to prevent lower back strain.*

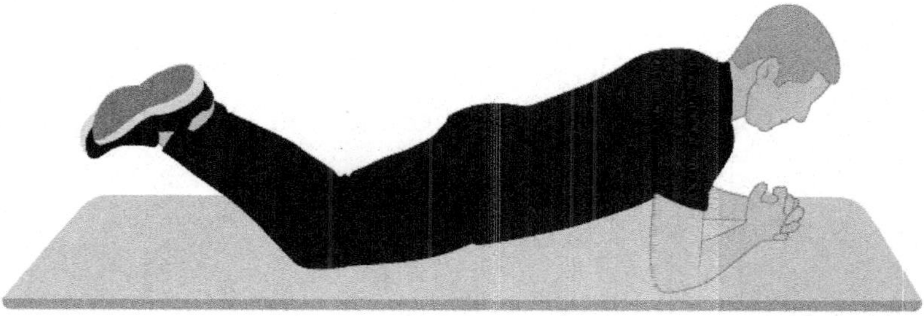

**SCAN FOR VIDEO**

## Crunch #40

As you learned in Chapter 7, the crunch has replaced the sit up as the safer way to work those abs and the rest of the core muscles.

---

- Lie on a mat or carpet with your head flat and your knees partially raised.
- Begin the crunch by raising your head, shoulders, and upper back 10 to 12 inches off the floor (unlike the sit-up, which reaches to your knees). As you rise, if you feel pain in your back, stop, and place a small folded towel under your lower back for support, then continue.
- Hold the crunch position for at least 2 to 3 seconds, tightening your core muscles, then slowly lower your head and shoulders to the bench to complete 1 rep. Do a total of 12 reps in the first set, rest for 30 seconds, and repeat for one more set.

**SCAN FOR VIDEO**

## Leg Raises #41

Despite the name, it's your core muscles—especially the abdominals—that benefit from leg raises.

- Lie on your back on a mat or carpet, with your legs fully extended. Slowly raise both legs with your knees slightly bent and continue raising until your feet are pointing to the ceiling. Pause, then slowly lower your legs to the mat for 1 rep. Continue raising and lowering your legs for a total of 10 reps.
- Tighten your abdominals to increase the effectiveness of the exercise.

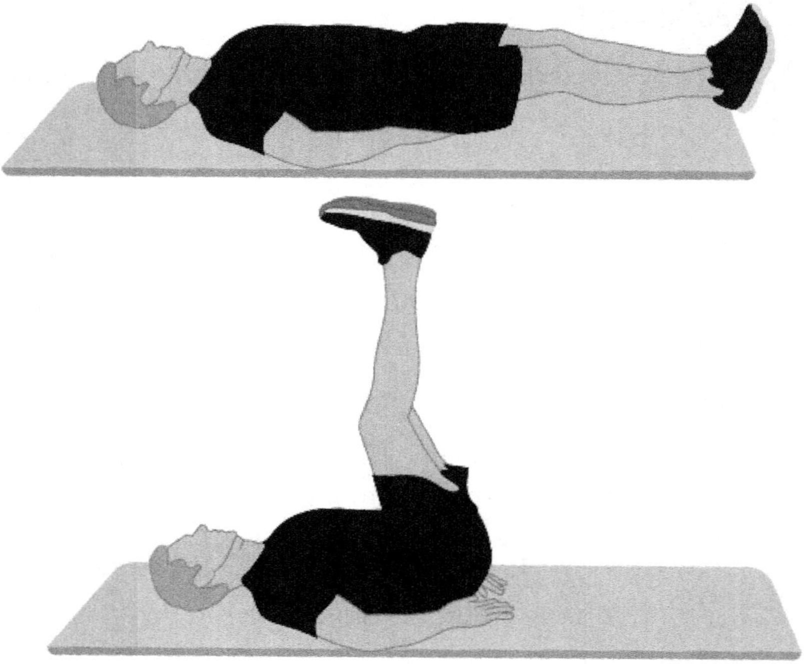

**SCAN FOR VIDEO**

## Modified Leg Raises

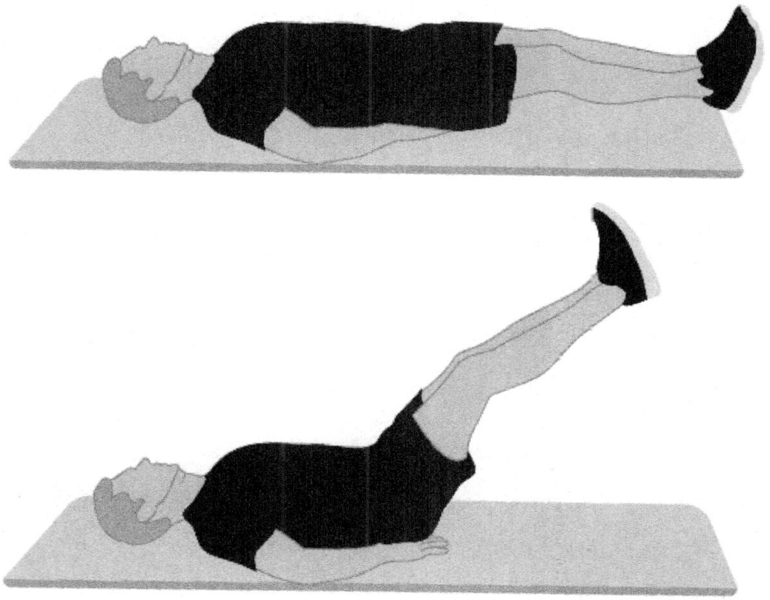

**SCAN FOR VIDEO**

## Squats #42

The thighs, especially your quadriceps, are the primary beneficiaries of squats, with some added effort attributed to your hamstrings, hip flexors, glutes, and calves.

---

- Stand upright with your feet about 12 to 14 inches apart and place your right hand on your left shoulder and left hand on the right shoulder. Begin by pushing your hips back as you bend your knees to lower your body, as if you are going to sit in a chair.
- Lean your body slightly forward from the hips, while keeping your back straight, without bending it. Be careful not to let your knees go forward past your toes.
- Pause for a moment, then rise back up to the standing position to complete 1 rep. Do 8 to 12 reps for one set; rest for 30 seconds, then perform a second set.
- *Note: It may be easier if you do the squats with your back against a wall, sliding down and back up.*

**SCAN FOR VIDEO**

## *Aerobic Exercises*

This is what all those joggers and cyclists are doing because it's great for heart health, and disease prevention overall. Your heart is a muscle, and aerobic or cardio training is how that muscle gets its exercise. It's also a good way to burn a good number of calories and help with weight control. Following a good aerobic workout, you'll often experience the rush of beta endorphin hormones, which are the cause of the so-called 'runner's high.'

## Aerobic Selection

In selecting which aerobic exercise to perform, keep in mind that these are for the long-term benefit of your health and well-being, so choose methods that you can stay with; in other words, don't take up jogging if you hate to run. And for that matter, if you are a senior, you'll be better off avoiding running on hard surfaces, or participating in any other high impact sport; your knees and joints will thank you.

- An aerobic workout can be achieved with a range of alternative activities, some of which can be done indoors on a treadmill, elliptical machine, or stair climber. You can also jump rope, and use an indoor stationary cycle. Or you can cycle outdoors, preferably in safe areas, and not in traffic with the danger of cars, and polluted air.

- If you have access to a pool, swimming is considered one of the most effective, risk-free forms of exercise. But this means doing laps, not splashing around.
- What about walking? Absolutely! It is low impact and can provide a good aerobic workout as long as it's done at a brisk pace, so that you are breathing deeply and your heart is pumping at a good rate—a subject we'll cover next.

## Your Aerobic Heart Rate

Extensive studies of cardiovascular conditioning have identified target heart rates based on age and your 'VO2 Max', the maximum heart rate you can achieve. Here's how it works:

Your estimated VO2 Max is the number 220 minus your age; you then take 65% of that to determine an ideal 'cruising pace' that you can comfortably sustain for most of your workout. Here's an example for a 50 year old person in normal health:

220 - 50 = 170 X 0.65 = 110

Now let's do this for someone who has reached age 70:

220 - 70 = 150 X 0.65 = 98

These calculations are approximate and are based on averages. If you are age 50, a steady workout pulse of 110 may feel easy, or you may find it too intense, and need to slow down. How you react is largely dependent on your level of conditioning; you must be the judge of how you feel.

- You can easily check your pulse by pressing your fingers into the left side of your neck, where the carotid artery can easily be found. Take a reading for 10 seconds, then multiply that by 6 to calculate your beats per minute, or 'BPM's.
- If you have a smartwatch or other wrist-monitor, it will give you a continuous reading, and show you the ideal rate range for your age.

Another guideline is to be able to speak and hold a conversation as you proceed through your aerobic workout. If you can speak, your breathing rate is in the safe range, but if you're nearly out of breath, and breathing with difficulty, ease up until your breathing is manageable. At the other extreme is when your pulse and breathing rates are too low, and you are not working hard enough, in which case it's time to pick up the pace.

**Meeting a top athlete:** He is playing at top performance levels despite being a senior, as far as pro sports go. His secret: A total-body resistance band workout, and it's coming up next.

**CHAPTER 9**

# A Top Athlete Tells You How

*The real glory is being knocked to your knees and then coming back. That's the essence of it.*

Vince Lombardi
football legend

## Learn From a Senior Who's Still Playing Tough

Consider this chapter a bonus; an extra, highly effective resistance band routine that you can easily learn and practice. This is the workout that Tom Brady uses to keep the top shape that allows him to still be a winning National Football League quarterback, well into his 40s.

Tom recently decided to retire, and then changed his mind, deciding to stay in the game. Why? His reasons may be personal, but one thing is for sure. He knew he could do it; that he was physically able to step onto the playing field and compete successfully among much younger players.

Tom Brady and I have a common goal: To help as many people as possible, especially seniors, to become stronger and healthier with more endurance and reliance, by staying physically active throughout their lives.

## *Warming Up*

As you've already read, it's important not to jump right into your resistance band workout without getting your heart to pump some extra oxygen-rich blood throughout your body, especially to your muscles.

If you can do a 10 minute cardio workout first, that's great, but if time or motivation is short, spend at least 5 minutes on a treadmill, stationary cycle, elliptical, or stair climber. If you're at home without access to those machines, do some running or hopping in place, interspersed with some yoga stretching, a few squats, some calf raises, maybe a few jumping jacks; anything that will warm you up. There are more instructions on warmups in Chapter 4's coverage for Beginners.

## A Full-Body Workout

### Tom Brady and You

These eight exercises, all performed with resistance bands, are the essentials of Tom Brady's full-body routine. He found that as he got older, his risks of injury with weights were increasing, and that he could stay in great shape with resistance bands. So can you!

You can choose to perform all of these exercises in one session, and assuming you've used sufficient resistance to really challenge your muscles, you should then rest for at least one day, or preferably two if you are a senior. So a Monday morning full-body workout should not be repeated before Wednesday or Thursday morning.

Alternatively, you can work your upper body including your arms, shoulders, and upper back on Monday; your midbody (abs and core) on Tuesday; and your lower body, from the hips, glutes, and thighs to calves and ankles on Wednesday. You'd then be ready to return to the upper body workout on Thursday.

As you perform this routine, the same guideline of two or three sets of 8 to 12 reps applies, with the last 1 or 2 reps in each set feeling challenging.

## Standing Row #43

This is a good way to wake up your upper body, and get your back, shoulder and arm muscles into gear, as you keep your lower body stable.

---

- Take a long looped band, and anchor one end to a door, or a pole, at about chest height. If you have tubes with handles, anchor an end of each. Take the other end of the band, or the handles in each hand, and step back with your arms extended forward until you feel tension in the band.
- Stand with your feet shoulder-width apart and bend your knees slightly; keep your upper body upright. Tighten your core and glutes, keeping your elbows close to your body, and begin the movement by pulling your hands to the sides of your chest in a rowing motion, pausing, then slowly extending your arms to return to the starting position.

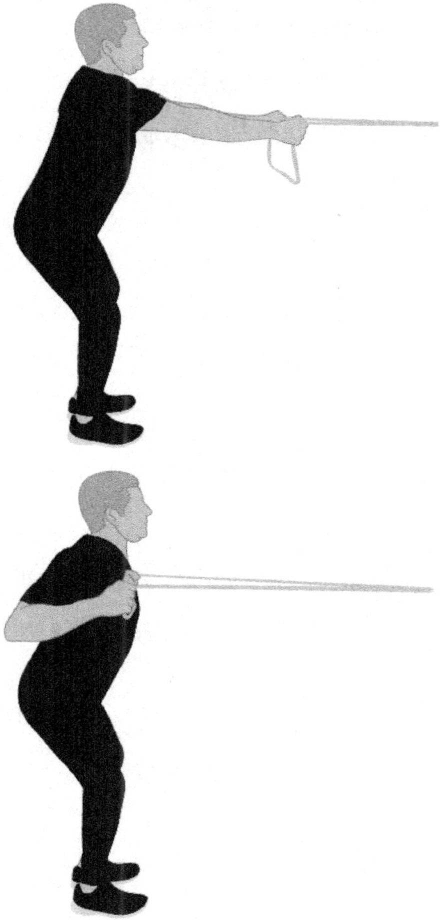

**SCAN FOR VIDEO**

## Banded Push Ups #44

***Banded push-ups are great exercise for your chest muscles, shoulders, and triceps.***

---

- Make sure to keep your back straight. Complete the first rep of the exercise by lowering your chest to the floor. Pause, then slowly rise back up to the starting position.
- The idea is to make the push up harder, so be sure to have a good amount of resistance in the band before you lower yourself. If you don't feel enough resistance, pull the band tighter.

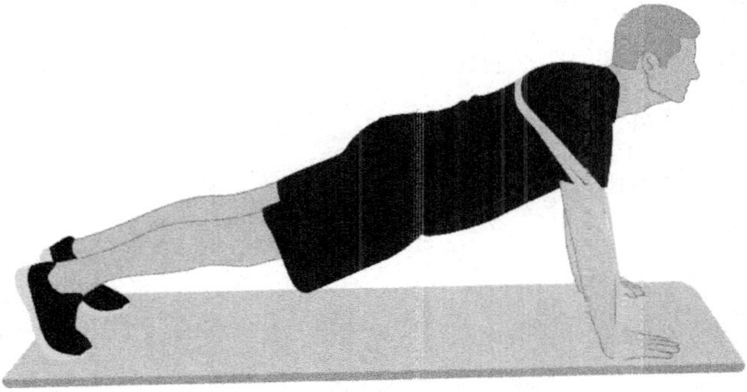

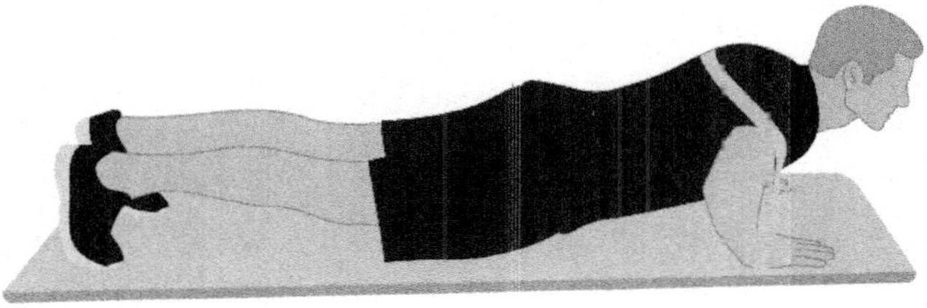

**SCAN FOR VIDEO**

## Core Rotations #45

This exercise will strengthen your abdominals and the side and back muscles of your core; it helps Tom to gain torque when he throws.

---

- Take the same stance as in the standing row, but now turn 45-degrees so you are holding the anchored band with your arms extended across your chest; your hands and arms should be pointing towards the anchor. Take a few side steps away from the anchor to make sure there's resistance in the bands.
- Begin by pulling the bands across your chest, and at the same time, turn your body away from the anchor, trying to have your back facing the anchor. Slowly turn back to the starting position, with your arms extended and pointing towards the anchor.

**SCAN FOR VIDEO**

## Biceps Curl 46

This is the definitive builder of your upper arm biceps muscles; the band's resistance takes the place of a traditional pair of dumbbells or a barbell. (This version offers the same benefits as the seated version in Chapter 6).

---

- Stand upright, keeping your back straight as you step on the center of a loop band, or, you may place each foot on the end of a flat band or tube. With your arms extended and pointing downward, there should be some light resistance felt in the bands; if not, adjust your grip and placement under your foot to tighten the band.
- Begin by raising both hands to your shoulders, keeping your elbow close to your body. Pause at the top of the movement, then slowly lower your hands and fully extend your arms downward; this completes your first rep. Remember to keep your back straight.

**SCAN FOR VIDEO**

## Triceps Extension #47

This exercise isolates and develops the triceps muscles at the rear of your upper arms; your shoulders will benefit as well.

---

- You'll need one long loop or two flat bands or tubes. Stand on the center of the loop or on the ends of the single bands or tubes and raise your hands behind your head. You should feel some, but not too much, resistance at this stage.
- Begin by raising your hands upwards, and *just behind your head*, with your elbows pointing forward. Extend your arms upward as fully as you are able. Pause at the top of the movement, then slowly lower your hands behind your head to complete 1 rep.

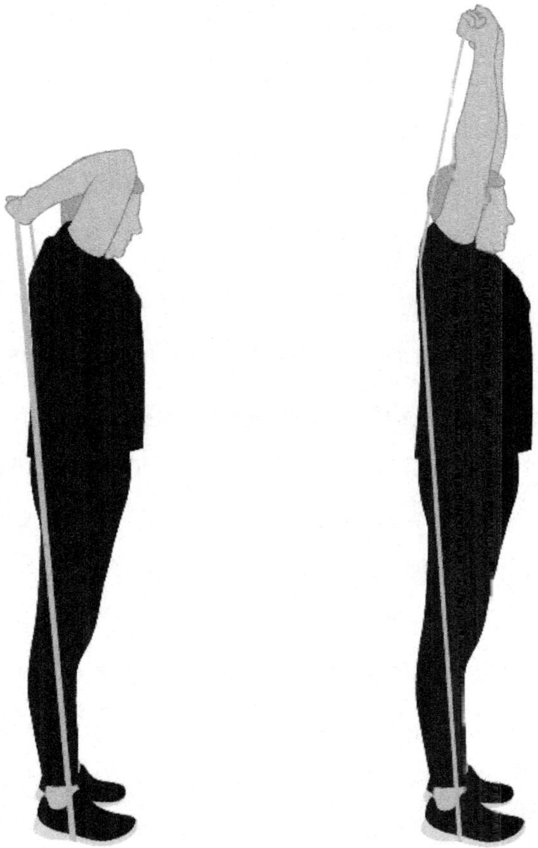

**SCAN FOR VIDEO**

## Banded Deceleration Lunges #48

These lunges are intensified by the band to further challenge your quadriceps, glutes, and hips.

---

- Loop a larger band around your waist and attach the other end to a door handle or post, making sure the connection will hold under tension.
- From a standing position, step backward with your right leg, and bend your right knee until it just touches the floor. Keeping your upper body as upright as you can, step back far enough that your left thigh is parallel to the floor. Pause, then rise back up to the starting position for your first rep.
- Do 8 to 10 reps, then switch legs and repeat the same number of reps with your left leg rearward to complete the first set.

**SCAN FOR VIDEO**

## Shoulder Press #49

This is almost the same as the Triceps Press, standing on a long loop or two flat bands or tubes, but with your hands held *in front of your shoulders*. You'll be pressing your hands and arms directly upward.

---

- Tighten your core and glutes and be sure there is sufficient resistance so that you have considerable tension when your arms are fully extended upward. Your hands should remain just forward of your head as you press upward, and your elbows should be pointing downward as you begin.
- Pause at the top of the movement, then slowly lower your hands to your shoulders to complete the first rep.

**SCAN FOR VIDEO**

## X-Band Squat #50

This is a good intensifier of the thigh-building squat exercise. You'll need both a short and a long loop band for this exercise.

---

- Step both feet into the short loop band and place it just above your knees. Step on the lower section of the large loop band with your feet shoulder-width apart. Twist the loop to form an X shape, and insert your head into the upper loop, and slide the band behind your neck. Press your hands together and push them forward to help your balance.
- Press your bum back and keep your body upright as you lower into a squat. Your knees should be above your toes, pointing forward, not inward. Tighten your core and glutes and be sure to press your knees outward to further engage the glutes and hips. Pause, then rise back up to standing posture to complete one rep.

SCAN FOR VIDEO

**Wrapping up:** The next and last chapters will keep you on the path of safety, good exercise practices, and how to follow a healthy, enjoyable dietary lifestyle practice.

**CHAPTER 10**

# Safety Tips, Good Practices, a Healthy Diet

*Our greatest ability as humans is not to change the world; but to change ourselves.*

Mahatma Gandhi

## Putting More Life in Your Years; More Years in Your Life

It's time to wrap up your resistance band training by ensuring you'll be able to perform your workouts safely and beneficially, and avoid the common injuries that anyone, but especially seniors, can experience when stressing joints and muscles.

In the spirit of the Hippocratic Oath's "First, do no harm," we begin with the basic ways to protect and strengthen your joints, and reduce the risks of injury. We then follow this with a summary of the good practices that will keep you from hurting yourself and enable you to make your fitness program a part of your daily routine, putting more years in your life, and more life in your years.

This chapter will conclude with a straightforward presentation of a healthy diet that you can adopt with ease and without sacrifice; a diet you'll love, and that will optimize your health and ability to stay fit.

## *Protect Your Joints: Safety Tips for Exercising as a Senior*

It is not a sign of weakness to acknowledge that your age will affect how you exercise. As a senior, the expression, "You're not a kid anymore" is of particular relevance when you put your joints, connective tissues, bones, and muscles through resistance training. No matter the exercise and dietary disciplines you have practiced, the years must be taken into account.

This means you are not as flexible as you once were and won't be able to bend or reach as deeply or as far as before. The flexibility of your muscles, ligaments, tendons, and joints gradually reduces as these connective tissues stiffen and become more resistant to stretching, as well as to the hard resistance work you're trying to impose. As a result:

**Your joints** are susceptible to injury as a result of reduced flexibility, strength and resilience, and longer recovery times. Virtually every movement we make involves flexing joints, from our fingers, hands, and wrists to our elbows, shoulders, neck, spine, hips, knees and ankles. We even have joints in our toes.

**Your recovery times** following a work out or any good amount of physical exertion will be longer. If you recall the concept of hypertrophy covered earlier, your muscle fibers and cells need time to repair and rebuild the damage to your muscles from these types of exertions. What used to take a day for recovery may take two or three days.

**You are not as strong or resilient** as you once were. If you could do bicep curls with a 25 lb or 30 lb dumbbell or resistance band equivalent when you were 35 years old, it is probably no longer possible if you are now 55 or 65; these days you may peak at 15 lb, or at most 20 lb.

**Your aerobic capacity** is also not what it once was, even if you've hit the trail or the treadmill faithfully for many years. As the data shows in the previous chapter, your optimal heart rate for sustaining a comfortable cardiovascular conditioning pace slows a little bit every year; adding up to six or seven *fewer beats per minute* every 10 years.

Furthermore, certain aerobic exercises can *damage your joints*, potentially permanently. Running, and other repetitive, sustained high impact activities can wear down the cartilage in your joints, especially knees and ankles; tennis can lead to tennis elbow, of course, and that abraded cartilage won't grow back!

**Your back is at risk.** We all experience back pain at certain times in our lives; it's as if the back is just waiting to inform us of its presence. There are many risks your upper and lower back can be exposed to, including dislocating spinal disks and pinching spinal nerves, causing sciatica. See the warning in the next section about lifting heavy objects with improper posture.

Okay, given those realities, what can you do to avoid injuries while getting into shape?

## Good Practices for Seniors

Let's extend the timeless maxim, "Know thyself, with Know thyself and thy physical limits." Be aware of your true capabilities, and don't push beyond them. Take care not to try to keep up with others, whose strength and conditioning may give them advantages; just be yourself and respect your limits.

- **Form and posture:** Learn how to do each movement correctly, and maintain good form, especially good posture. Be attentive to the instructions for each movement, and don't try shortcuts or fast movements to get through the exercise quickly. Slower is better by being safer, and also more productive in creating resistance to make you stronger.
- **Lift responsibly:** This includes *all lifting* you may do, whether it's during your resistance bands workout, or when moving a dresser or hauling a heavy box. Bend your knees, keep your back straight without arching or bending your spine, and use your thighs to push yourself up. (This is why it's important to practice squats, and to do so correctly!)
- **Don't powerlift:** Avoid trying to lift or pull heavier resistance than you can handle, and don't try powerlifting, which involves resistance that is so intense that only 1 or 2 reps can be performed in a set. This may build bigger muscles when the person is young, but for seniors, it's a recipe for pulls, strains, and tears. You should be able to do at least 8 reps for the resistance level to be safe for you.

- **Safety first:** Be attentive to safety concerns when using your resistance bands and tubes. Take an extra few moments when attaching one end of the band to a stationary object, and ensure the band, or its handle, will not come loose and snap back and hit you in the face. If you are hooking the handle at the end of a tube, secure it with another band or strap.
- **Protect your equipment:** Make sure you are not exposing the bands and tubes to sharp or rough, abrasive surfaces, such as when placing the band over the top of a door, or a tree branch. Be careful when tying bands together to extend them or create a loop; use a slipknot so the knot can be untied, but make sure it will hold during use. Read the safety instructions that come with the equipment.
- **Get help:** If you have any doubts about how to use resistance bands and tubes, consult a trainer who is familiar with them (but not a trainer who will steer you away from bands and over to weightlifting!). Be attentive to the instructions you receive, especially when the trainer shows you how to stand and maintain good posture, and how to do each movement.

- **See your doctor:** Finally, as you've been advised throughout the book, if you are new to exercise, or if it's been quite a while since you were in shape, get checked out medically before starting resistance and aerobic exercises. In the same spirit, get medical help if you experience serious pain during a workout; it may just be fatigue or a slight strain, but it's best to rule out anything serious, and attend to it immediately if necessary.

## *What About Diet?*

Yes, what you eat (and how much) is essential to health and fitness, and we'll give you the lowdown on a diet endorsed by the medical professionals at the Mayo Clinic, Harvard Medical School, Johns Hopkins, and the Cleveland Clinic, especially for protecting heart health. "In January, US News and World Report named it the 'best diet overall' for the second year running" (Harvard Health, 2019). It's based on healthy, delicious foods, so you can ignore all those fad diets and go with the diet recognized by medical authorities to help you live your longest and best.

## The Mediterranean Diet

The residents of the Mediterranean Basin live longer and healthier lives than worldwide average expectancies, and the consensus among cardiologists, and other medical professionals, is that these advantages trace to the quality and nature of their diets, along with being physically active and socially interactive.

You can learn about this diet, and find many good recipes online; Here is a brief summary of the components and benefits of the Mediterranean diet, profiled by WebMD (2022):

- **Heart healthy:** "Almost everything in this diet is good for your heart. Olive oil and nuts help lower 'bad' LDL cholesterol. Fruits, veggies, and beans help keep arteries clear." Fish from coldwater sources like salmon, tuna, and sardines help lower triglycerides and blood pressure. "Even a daily glass of wine may be good for your heart!" (More on this below).
- **No calorie counting:** Instead, trade heart-healthy fats like olive oil for unhealthy fats like butter, margarine, and shortening. Fish and lean poultry are healthier than saturated fats in red meat and full-fat dairy products. Have sweet-tasting, vitamin and fiber-rich fresh fruit, and avoid the empty

calories in sugar-laden desserts. You can have dark chocolate, but in moderate amounts.

- **Veggies unlimited:** Enjoy as much as you want of flavorful vegetables and salad greens, and you can also enjoy whole grains and beans. Nuts of every type, and seeds, like chia, flax, pumpkin, and sunflower, are great for you, but stick to a handful a day, since they're oil rich.
- **Avoid salty prepared foods:** like bacon and sausages, and canned, preserved meats that are low in nutrients, and focus on "Seasonal food that's made in simple, mouth-watering ways. Build a yummy salad from spinach, cucumbers, and tomatoes." Choose a diversity of colors for your salad for optimal minerals and vitamins.
- **Bread is back:** It's now recognized as good for you. But only if you choose breads made with whole grains, which have more protein, fiber, and minerals and are healthier than breads made with white flour. "Try whole-grain pita bread dipped in olive oil, hummus, or tahini, a protein-rich paste made from ground sesame seeds."
- **Eggs are back too:** and are recommended in moderation, given their quality protein and low saturated fats. One a day, or no more than about

eight per week is okay with the cardiologists! Use little or no butter when cooking to keep saturated fat intake low.

- **Go easy on the salt:** and add spices for safer, better flavors. Drop in some bay leaves, sauteed onion, rosemary, coriander, cilantro, pepper, and cinnamon to add lots of flavor, so you can cut back on hypertension-causing salt. Many spices and herbs "Have health benefits, too; coriander and rosemary, for example, have disease-fighting antioxidants and nutrients."
- **More about wine:** A glass or two taken with meals is "Common in many Mediterranean countries, where dining is often leisurely and social." There's evidence that "One glass a day for women and two for men may be good for your heart. Talk to your doctor to see if it's a good idea for you." Other sources of alcohol—beer and distilled spirits—may also be beneficial if similarly consumed in moderation.
- **You won't be hungry:** because you'll be eating rich-tasting foods like "Roasted sweet potatoes, hummus, and even lima bean spread." These and other complex carbohydrates tend to digest slowly, letting you feel full for a longer time. In addition, "Hunger's not a problem when you can munch on

nuts, olives, or bites of low-fat cheese when a craving strikes." Just don't overeat!

- **Get smarter:** The nutrition that's good for your heart is also beneficial for your brain. By consuming antioxidant-rich foods and avoiding "bad fats and processed foods which can cause inflammation," you are making "this eating style a brain-friendly choice."

## The DASH Diet

You may have heard of this medically endorsed diet; DASH stands for *Dietary Approaches to Stop Hypertension*, and its primary target group are those at risk for high blood pressure, and strokes this condition can lead to.

- DASH is very similar to the Mediterranean diet, with one important exception: it limits salt intake, since the sodium in salt directly affects blood pressure.
- Apart from this one distinction, DASH diets emphasize vegetables and fruits, whole grains, nuts and seeds, beans, low fat dairy, eggs, coldwater fish, less red meat, and no processed meats, like Spam, bacon, and sausages, all of which are commonly high in sodium.
- "DASH diet and Mediterranean diet are the most popular diet plans in the US. As per World Health

Report and US News, both have been declared the top 2 best eating plans consistently over the years," reports Sarika Moghe in *Health Unplugged* (2022).

- If hypertension is a concern, be sure to read labels and check the sodium content. Many canned foods are high in salt, but some offer low-salt versions.

## You've Made It!

You have now mastered the exercises within Resistance Bands For Seniors 50, 60 and Beyond – **Congratulations!**

This completes your resistance band training. Now on to Chapter 11: **Workout Programs**

To provide further encouragement we have designed 4 week workout routines specifically for you. They are intended to help you build a habit of regular exercise.

Initially, the workouts are to be performed twice a week. As your fitness and strength increase, consider working out more frequently, increasing the number of repetitions performed or using stronger Bands and when you feel ready and confident move to the next level workouts.

These whole body workouts are suggestions only. You can modify each workout to suit your particular interest.

***The most important thing to achieve your goal is consistency.***

**Exercise regularly and you will see your strength and fitness improve!**

CHAPTER 11

# Workout Programs

*"what seems impossible today will one day become your warm-up."*

## Exercise Videos

It is often beneficial and easier to see an exercise being performed rather than following written instructions. Which is why, each exercise in this book has a QR code that links to it's video clip.

While all the exercises included in each workout routine below can be accessed individually by scanning their respective QR codes, **if you wish to see all the exercises included in a workout in a single video**, avoiding the necessity of scanning each exercise's QR code one at a time, become part of our community by scanning this QR code.

## 4 Week Workouts

Here we'll cover four different types of workouts you can do to keep things mixed up, so your body will end up constantly adapting, avoiding plateaus in your progress:

- Beginner's Workouts
- Intermediate Workouts
- Advanced Workouts
- Seated Workouts

See the next page for the programs ...

# Beginner Workout (4 weeks)

## Beginner - Week 1 (a)

| Exercise | # | Sets | Reps | Rest |
|---|---|---|---|---|
| Chest Pull Apart | **#1** | 3 | 10 | 30 seconds |
| Lat Pulldown | **#2** | 3 | 10 | 30 seconds |
| Band Side Step | **#5** | 3 | 30 seconds | 30 seconds |
| Clamshell | **#6** | 2 (each side) | 10 | 30 seconds |
| Pallof Press | **#4** | 2 | 5 (each side) | 30 seconds |

## Beginner - Week 1 (b)

| Exercise | # | Sets | Reps | Rest |
|---|---|---|---|---|
| Chest Press | **#8** | 3 | 10 | 30 seconds |
| Seated Row | **#3** | 3 | 10 | 30 seconds |
| Band Side Step | **#5** | 3 | 30 seconds | 30 seconds |
| Side Leg Lift | **#7** | 2 (each side) | 10 | 30 seconds |
| Pallof Press | **#4** | 2 | 5 (each side) | 30 seconds |

## Beginner - Week 2 (a)

| Exercise | # | Sets | Reps | Rest |
|---|---|---|---|---|
| Chest Pull Apart | **#1** | 3 | 10-12 | 30 seconds |
| Lat Pulldown | **#2** | 3 | 10-12 | 30 seconds |
| Band Side Step | **#5** | 3 | 35 seconds | 30 seconds |
| Clamshell | **#6** | 2 (each side) | 10-12 | 30 seconds |
| Pallof Press | **#4** | 2 | 6 (each side) | 30 seconds |

## Beginner - Week 2 (b)

| Exercise | # | Sets | Reps | Rest |
|---|---|---|---|---|
| Chest Press | **#1** | 3 | 10-12 | 30 seconds |
| Seated Row | **#3** | 3 | 10-12 | 30 seconds |
| Band Side Step | **#5** | 3 | 35 seconds | 30 seconds |
| Side Leg Lift | **#7** | 2 (each side) | 10-12 | 30 seconds |
| Pallof Press | **#4** | 2 | 6 (each side) | 30 seconds |

## Beginner - Week 3 (a)

| Exercise | # | Sets | Reps | Rest |
|---|---|---|---|---|
| Chest Pull Apart | **#1** | 3 | 12-15 | 30 seconds |
| Lat Pulldown | **#2** | 3 | 12-15 | 30 seconds |
| Band Side Step | **#5** | 3 | 40 seconds | 30 seconds |
| Clamshell | **#6** | 2 (each side) | 12-15 | 30 seconds |
| Pallof Press | **#4** | 2 | 7 (each side) | 30 seconds |

## Beginner - Week 3 (b)

| Exercise | # | Sets | Reps | Rest |
|---|---|---|---|---|
| Chest Press | **#8** | 3 | 12-15 | 30 seconds |
| Seated Row | **#3** | 3 | 12-15 | 30 seconds |
| Band Side Step | **#5** | 3 | 40 seconds | 30 seconds |
| Side Leg Lift | **#7** | 2 (each side) | 12-15 | 30 seconds |
| Pallof Press | **#4** | 2 | 7 (each side) | 30 seconds |

## Beginner - Week 4 (a)

| Exercise | # | Sets | Reps | Rest |
|---|---|---|---|---|
| Chest Pull Apart | **#1** | 3 | 12-20 | 30 seconds |
| Lat Pulldown | **#2** | 3 | 12-20 | 30 seconds |
| Band Side Step | **#5** | 3 | 45 seconds | 30 seconds |
| Clamshell | **#6** | 2 (each side) | 12-20 | 30 seconds |
| Pallof Press | **#4** | 2 | 8 (each side) | 30 seconds |

## Beginner - Week 4 (b)

| Exercise | # | Sets | Reps | Rest |
|---|---|---|---|---|
| Chest Press | **#8** | 3 | 12-20 | 30 seconds |
| Seated Row | **#3** | 3 | 12-20 | 30 seconds |
| Band Side Step | **#5** | 3 | 45 seconds | 30 seconds |
| Side Leg Lift | **#7** | 2 (each side) | 12-20 | 30 seconds |
| Pallof Press | **#4** | 2 | 8 (each side) | 30 seconds |

# Intermediate Workout (4 weeks)

## Intermediate - Week 1 (a)

| Exercise | # | Sets | Reps | Rest |
|---|---|---|---|---|
| Hip Thrust | **#9** | 3 | 10-15 | 30 seconds |
| Bulgarian Split Squat | **#10** | 3 (each side) | 10 | 30 seconds |
| Bend Over | **#15** | 3 | 10-20 | 30 seconds |
| Banded Push Up | **#12** | 3 | 8-12 | 30 seconds |
| One Arm Row | **#14** | 3 (each side) | 10 | 30 seconds |
| One Arm Shoulder Press | **#13** | 3 (each arm) | 10 | 30 seconds |

## Intermediate - Week 1 (b)

| Exercise | # | Sets | Reps | Rest |
|---|---|---|---|---|
| Hip Thrust | **#9** | 3 | 10-20 | 30 seconds |
| Bulgarian Split Squat | **#10** | 3 (each side) | 10 | 30 seconds |
| Pull Down | **#11** | 3 | 10 | 30 seconds |
| Banded Push Up | **#12** | 3 | 8-12 | 30 seconds |
| Banded Dead Bug | **#16** | 2 (each side) | 12 | 30 seconds |
| Banded Plank Walk | **#17** | 3 | 10 | 30 seconds |

## Intermediate - Week 2 (a)

| Exercise | # | Sets | Reps | Rest |
|---|---|---|---|---|
| Hip Thrust | **#9** | 3 | 12-15 | 30 seconds |
| Bulgarian Split Squat | **#10** | 3 (each side) | 12 | 30 seconds |
| Bend Over | **#15** | 3 | 15-20 | 30 seconds |
| Banded Push Up | **#12** | 3 | 10-12 | 30 seconds |
| One Arm Row | **#14** | 3 (each side) | 12 | 30 seconds |
| One Arm Shoulder Press | **#13** | 3 (each arm) | 12 | 30 seconds |

## Intermediate - Week 2 (b)

| Exercise | # | Sets | Reps | Rest |
|---|---|---|---|---|
| Hip Thrust | **#9** | 3 | 12-20 | 30 seconds |
| Bulgarian Split Squat | **#10** | 3 (each side) | 12 | 30 seconds |
| Pull Down | **#11** | 3 | 12-15 | 30 seconds |
| Banded Push Up | **#12** | 3 | 10-12 | 30 seconds |
| Banded Dead Bug | **#16** | 2 (each side) | 15 | 30 seconds |
| Banded Plank Walk | **#17** | 3 | 12 | 30 seconds |

## Intermediate - Week 3 (a)

| Exercise | # | Sets | Reps | Rest |
|---|---|---|---|---|
| Hip Thrust | **#9** | 3 | 15 | 30 seconds |
| Bulgarian Split Squat | **#10** | 3 (each side) | 15 | 30 seconds |
| Bend Over | **#15** | 3 | 20 | 30 seconds |

| Exercise | # | Sets | Reps | Rest |
|---|---|---|---|---|
| Banded Push Up | **#12** | 3 | 12 | 30 seconds |
| One Arm Row | **#14** | 3 (each side) | 12-15 | 30 seconds |
| One Arm Shoulder Press | **#13** | 3 (each arm) | 12-15 | 30 seconds |

## Intermediate - Week 3 (b)

| Exercise | # | Sets | Reps | Rest |
|---|---|---|---|---|
| Hip Thrust | **#9** | 3 | 20 | 30 seconds |
| Bulgarian Split Squat | **#10** | 3 (each side) | 15 | 30 seconds |
| Pull Down | **#11** | 3 | 15 | 30 seconds |
| Banded Push Up | **#12** | 3 | 12 | 30 seconds |
| Banded Dead Bug | **#16** | 2 (each side) | 15-20 | 30 seconds |
| Banded Plank Walk | **#17** | 3 | 12 | 30 seconds |

## Intermediate - Week 4 (a)

| Exercise | # | Sets | Reps | Rest |
|---|---|---|---|---|
| Hip Thrust | **#9** | 3 | 15-20 | 30 seconds |
| Bulgarian Split Squat | **#10** | 3 (each side) | 15 | 30 seconds |
| Bend Over | **#15** | 3 | 20 | 30 seconds |
| Banded Push Up | **#12** | 3 | 12-15 | 30 seconds |
| One Arm Row | **#14** | 3 (each side) | 15 | 30 seconds |
| One Arm Shoulder Press | **#13** | 3 (each arm) | 15 | 30 seconds |

## Intermediate - Week 4 (b)

| Exercise | # | Sets | Reps | Rest |
|---|---|---|---|---|
| Hip Thrust | **#9** | 3 | 20 | 30 seconds |
| Bulgarian Split Squat | **#10** | 3 (each side) | 15 | 30 seconds |
| Pull Down | **#11** | 3 | 15-20 | 30 seconds |
| Banded Push Up | **#12** | 3 | 12-15 | 30 seconds |
| Banded Dead Bug | **#16** | 2 (each side) | 20 | 30 seconds |
| Banded Plank Walk | **#17** | 3 | 15 | 30 seconds |

# Advanced Workout (4 weeks)

## Advanced Workout - Week 1 (a)

| Exercise | # | Sets | Reps | Rest |
|---|---|---|---|---|
| Pull to Face | **#30** | 3 | 12-20 | 30 seconds |
| Front Squat | **#31** | 3 | 8-12 | 60 seconds |
| Single Leg Deadlift | **#32** | 3 (each side) | 10 | 60 seconds |
| Bulgarian Split Squat | **#10** | 3 (each side) | 10 | 40 seconds |
| Hip Thrust | **#9** | 3 | 10-15 | 30 seconds |
| Chest Crossover | **#35** | 3 | 10-15 | 30 seconds |
| Lateral Raise | **#37** | 3 | 10-12 | 30 seconds |
| One Arm Row | **#14** | 3 (each side) | 10 | 30 seconds |
| Resistance Crunch | **#36** | 3 | 8 | 30 seconds |

## Advanced Workout - Week 1 (b)

| Exercise | # | Sets | Reps | Rest |
|---|---|---|---|---|
| Pull to Face | **#30** | 3 | 12-20 | 30 seconds |
| Clean and Press | **#33** | 4 | 6-10 | 60 seconds |
| Hip Thrust | **#9** | 3 | 10-20 | 30 seconds |
| Bulgarian Split Squat | **#10** | 3 (each side) | 10 | 60 seconds |
| Chest Press | **#8** | 3 | 10 | 30 seconds |
| Lat Pulldown | **#2** | 3 | 8-12 | 30 seconds |
| Bear Crawl | **#34** | 3 | 10 | 60 seconds |
| Pallof Press | **#4** | 2 | 10 (each side) | 40 seconds |
| Banded Plank Walk | **#17** | 3 | 10 | 30 seconds |

## Advanced Workout - Week 2 (a)

| Exercise | # | Sets | Reps | Rest |
|---|---|---|---|---|
| Pull to Face | **#30** | 3 | 15-20 | 30 seconds |
| Front Squat | **#31** | 3 | 10-12 | 60 seconds |
| Single Leg Deadlift | **#32** | 3 (each side) | 10-12 | 60 seconds |
| Bulgarian Split Squat | **#10** | 3 (each side) | 10-15 | 40 seconds |
| Hip Thrust | **#9** | 3 | 10-20 | 30 seconds |
| Chest Crossover | **#35** | 3 | 15 | 30 seconds |
| Lateral Raise | **#37** | 3 | 12 | 30 seconds |
| One Arm Row | **#14** | 3 (each side) | 10-15 | 30 seconds |
| Resistance Crunch | **#36** | 3 | 8-10 | 30 seconds |

## Advanced Workout - Week 2 (b)

| Exercise | # | Sets | Reps | Rest |
|---|---|---|---|---|
| Pull to Face | **#30** | 3 | 15-20 | 30 seconds |
| Clean and Press | **#33** | 4 | 8-10 | 60 seconds |
| Hip Thrust | **#9** | 3 | 15-20 | 30 seconds |
| Bulgarian Split Squat | **#10** | 3 (each side) | 10-12 | 60 seconds |
| Chest Press | **#8** | 3 | 10-15 | 30 seconds |
| Lat Pulldown | **#2** | 3 | 10-12 | 30 seconds |
| Bear Crawl | **#34** | 3 | 10-12 | 60 seconds |
| Pallof Press | **#4** | 2 | 12 (each side) | 40 seconds |
| Banded Plank Walk | **#17** | 3 | 15 | 30 seconds |

## Advanced Workout - Week 3 (a)

| Exercise | # | Sets | Reps | Rest |
|---|---|---|---|---|
| Pull to Your Face | **#30** | 3 | 20 | 30 seconds |
| Front Squat | **#31** | 3 | 12-15 | 60 seconds |
| Single Leg Deadlift | **#32** | 3 (each side) | 12-15 | 60 seconds |
| Bulgarian Split Squat | **#10** | 3 (each side) | 15 | 40 seconds |
| Hip Thrust | **#9** | 3 | 15-20 | 30 seconds |
| Chest Crossover | **#35** | 3 | 15-20 | 30 seconds |
| Lateral Leg Raise | **#37** | 3 | 12-15 | 30 seconds |
| One Arm Row | **#14** | 3 (each side) | 12-15 | 30 seconds |
| Resistance Crunch | **#36** | 3 | 10-15 | 30 seconds |

## Advanced Workout - Week 3 (b)

| Exercise | # | Sets | Reps | Rest |
|---|---|---|---|---|
| Pull to Face | **#30** | 3 | 20 | 30 seconds |
| Clean and Press | **#33** | 4 | 10-12 | 60 seconds |
| Hip Thrust | **#9** | 3 | 20 | 30 seconds |
| Bulgarian Split Squat | **#10** | 3 (each side) | 12-15 | 60 seconds |
| Chest Press | **#8** | 3 | 15-20 | 30 seconds |
| Lat Pulldown | **#2** | 3 | 10-15 | 30 seconds |
| Bear Crawl | **#34** | 3 | 10-15 | 60 seconds |
| Pallof Press | **#4** | 2 | 15 (each side) | 40 seconds |
| Banded Plank Walk | **#17** | 3 | 15-20 | 30 seconds |

## Advanced Workout - Week 4 (a)

| Exercise | # | Sets | Reps | Rest |
|---|---|---|---|---|
| Pull to Face | **#30** | 3 | 20 | 30 seconds |
| Front Squat | **#31** | 3 | 15-20 | 60 seconds |
| Single Leg Deadlift | **#32** | 3 (each side) | 15 | 60 seconds |
| Bulgarian Split Squat | **#10** | 3 (each side) | 15 | 40 seconds |
| Hip Thrust | **#9** | 3 | 20 | 30 seconds |
| Chest Crossover | **#35** | 3 | 20 | 30 seconds |
| Lateral Leg Raise | **#37** | 3 | 15 | 30 seconds |
| One Arm Row | **#14** | 3 (each side) | 15-20 | 30 seconds |
| Resistance Crunch | **#36** | 3 | 10-20 | 30 seconds |

## Advanced Workout - Week 4 (b)

| Exercise | # | Sets | Reps | Rest |
|---|---|---|---|---|
| Pull to Face | **#30** | 3 | 20 | 30 seconds |
| Clean and Press | **#33** | 4 | 12 | 60 seconds |
| Hip Thrust | **#9** | 3 | 20 | 30 seconds |
| Bulgarian Split Squat | **#10** | 3 (each side) | 15 | 60 seconds |
| Chest Press | **#8** | 3 | 20 | 30 seconds |
| Lat Pulldown | **#2** | 3 | 15-20 | 30 seconds |
| Bear Crawl | **#34** | 3 | 15 | 60 seconds |
| Pallof Press | **#4** | 2 | 20 (each side) | 40 seconds |
| Banded Plank Walk | **#17** | 3 | 20 | 30 seconds |

# Seated Workouts (4 weeks)

## Seated Workouts - Week 1 (a)

| Exercise | # | Sets | Reps | Rest |
|---|---|---|---|---|
| Chest Press | **#23** | 3 | 10-12 | 30 seconds |
| Shoulder Press | **#24** | 3 | 10-12 | 30 seconds |
| Tricep Extension 1 | **#25** | 2-3 (each side) | 8-10 | 30 seconds |
| Bicep Curl 1 | **#27** | 3 (each side) | 8-10 | 30 seconds |
| Leg Press | **#20** | 3 (each leg) | 5-10 | 30 seconds |
| Leg Lift | **#19** | 3 (each leg) | 5 | 30 seconds |
| Pointed Foot Flex | **#18** | 3 (each leg) | 5 | 30 seconds |
| Abdominal Lean | **#22** | 3 | 10 | 30 seconds |

## Seated Workouts – Week 1 (b)

| Exercise | # | Sets | Reps | Rest |
|---|---|---|---|---|
| Chest Stretch | **#29** | 2-3 | 10 | 30 seconds |
| Shoulder Press | **#24** | 3 | 10-12 | 30 seconds |
| Tricep Extension 2 | **#26** | 2-3 (each side) | 8-10 | 30 seconds |
| Bicep Curl 2 | **#28** | 3 (each side) | 8-10 | 30 seconds |
| Hip Opener | **#21** | 3 (each leg) | 5-8 | 30 seconds |
| Leg Lift | **#19** | 3 (each leg) | 5 | 30 seconds |
| Pointed Toes | **#18** | 3 (each leg) | 5 | 30 seconds |
| Abdominal Lean | **#22** | 3 | 10 | 30 seconds |

## Seated Workouts - Week 2 (a)

| Exercise | # | Sets | Reps | Rest |
|---|---|---|---|---|
| Chest Press | **#23** | 3 | 12 | 30 seconds |
| Shoulder Press | **#24** | 3 | 12 | 30 seconds |
| Tricep Extension 1 | **#25** | 2-3 (each side) | 10 | 30 seconds |
| Bicep Curl 1 | **#27** | 3 (each side) | 10 | 30 seconds |
| Leg Press | **#20** | 3 (each leg) | 8-10 | 30 seconds |
| Leg Lift | **#19** | 3 (each leg) | 6 | 30 seconds |
| Pointed Toes | **#18** | 3 (each leg) | 6 | 30 seconds |
| Abdominal Lean | **#22** | 3 | 15 | 30 seconds |

## Seated Workouts – Week 2 (b)

| Exercise | # | Sets | Reps | Rest |
|---|---|---|---|---|
| Chest Stretch | **#29** | 2-3 | 10-15 | 30 seconds |
| Shoulder Press | **#24** | 3 | 12 | 30 seconds |
| Tricep Extension 2 | **#26** | 2-3 (each side) | 10 | 30 seconds |
| Bicep Curl 2 | **#28** | 3 (each side) | 10 | 30 seconds |
| Hip Opener | **#21** | 3 (each leg) | 8-10 | 30 seconds |
| Leg Lift | **#19** | 3 (each leg) | 6 | 30 seconds |
| Pointed Toes | **#18** | 3 (each leg) | 6 | 30 seconds |
| Abdominal Lean | **#22** | 3 | 15 | 30 seconds |

## Seated Workouts – Week 3 (a)

| Exercise | # | Sets | Reps | Rest |
|---|---|---|---|---|
| Chest Press | **#23** | 3 | 12-15 | 30 seconds |
| Shoulder Press | **#24** | 3 | 12-15 | 30 seconds |
| Tricep Extension 1 | **#25** | 2-3 (each side) | 10-12 | 30 seconds |
| Bicep Curl 1 | **#27** | 3 (each side) | 10-12 | 30 seconds |
| Leg Press | **#20** | 3 (each leg) | 10 | 30 seconds |
| Leg Lift | **#19** | 3 (each leg) | 6-8 | 30 seconds |
| Pointed Toes | **#18** | 3 (each leg) | 6-8 | 30 seconds |
| Abdominal Lean | **#22** | 3 | 15-20 | 30 seconds |

## Seated Workouts – Week 3 (b)

| Exercise | # | Sets | Reps | Rest |
|---|---|---|---|---|
| Chest Stretch | **#29** | 2-3 | 15-20 | 30 seconds |
| Shoulder Press | **#24** | 3 | 12-15 | 30 seconds |
| Tricep Extension 2 | **#26** | 2-3 (each side) | 10-12 | 30 seconds |
| Bicep Curl 2 | **#28** | 3 (each side) | 10-12 | 30 seconds |
| Hip Opener | **#21** | 3 (each leg) | 10 | 30 seconds |
| Leg Lift | **#19** | 3 (each leg) | 6-8 | 30 seconds |
| Pointed Toes | **#18** | 3 (each leg) | 6-8 | 30 seconds |
| Abdominal Lean | **#22** | 3 | 15-20 | 30 seconds |

## Seated Workouts – Week 4 (a)

| **Exercise** | **#** | **Sets** | **Reps** | **Rest** |
|---|---|---|---|---|
| Chest Press | **#23** | 3 | 15 | 30 seconds |
| Shoulder Press | **#24** | 3 | 15 | 30 seconds |
| Tricep Extension 1 | **#25** | 2-3 (each side) | 12 | 30 seconds |
| Bicep Curl 1 | **#27** | 3 (each side) | 12 | 30 seconds |
| Leg Press | **#20** | 3 (each leg) | 10-15 | 30 seconds |
| Leg Lift | **#19** | 3 (each leg) | 8 | 30 seconds |
| Pointed Toes | **#18** | 3 (each leg) | 8 | 30 seconds |
| Abdominal Lean | **#22** | 3 | 20 | 30 seconds |

## Seated Workouts – Week 4 (b)

| **Exercise** | **#** | **Sets** | **Reps** | **Rest** |
|---|---|---|---|---|
| Chest Stretch | **#29** | 2-3 | 20 | 30 seconds |
| Shoulder Press | **#24** | 3 | 15 | 30 seconds |
| Tricep Extension 2 | **#26** | 2-3 (each side) | 12 | 30 seconds |
| Bicep Curl 2 | **#28** | 3 (each side) | 12 | 30 seconds |
| Hip Opener | **#21** | 3 (each leg) | 10-12 | 30 seconds |
| Leg Lift | **#19** | 3 (each leg) | 8 | 30 seconds |
| Pointed Toes | **#18** | 3 (each leg) | 8 | 30 seconds |
| Abdominal Lean | **#22** | 3 | 20 | 30 seconds |

# CHAPTER 12

# Conclusion

## The Great Equalizer

Resistance bands represent what you could call 'The Great Equalizer' among the muscle and strength building alternatives. Resistance bands are accessible to virtually everyone, and are far less expensive than owning weightlifting equipment, or joining a fitness center. They are portable, easy to store, and can be used at home, or just about anywhere.

Yet resistance bands are equal to the weights and cable machines in building muscle mass, strength, and endurance:

- Performing 10 to 12 tricep presses, bicep curls, chest presses, or any other muscle-building movements with resistance bands and tubes will give the same results as the same movements with dumbbells and barbells, assuming equivalent resistance levels.

- You can replicate what you could do in a well-equipped gym with the many resistance band exercises we've covered in this book, and actually go farther and do more than most gym workouts entail.
- Resistance bands may be actually more effective than weights, because the intensity of the resistance increases as you lift or pull; weights tend to 'weigh less' when you get to the top of the lift. Your bands, conversely, intensify the challenge.
- Bodyweight calisthenics are a good supplement to resistance band training, because they too can be performed anywhere, without the costs and inconveniences of equipment. Even better, in combination, resistance bands and calisthenics can optimize the results of your workouts.

**Consider your safety:** As a senior, you will appreciate that resistance bands are credited with being safer than weights. You won't injure yourself by dropping a weight or losing control of it so it pulls or tears a muscle or tendon, or yanks a joint out of place. You will be less likely to lift or pull too heavy a resistance level, and over-exhaust your muscles.

**Mind your form:** Effectiveness in getting stronger and doing it safely means being attentive to the instructions for each individual move. Make sure your form is correct and you're always maintaining good posture in order to reinforce it, rather than compromising the exercises and reinforcing bad posture!

**Protect your back:** Be especially attentive to your back, which you depend on continuously, and which is easily injured if you are careless when working out with resistance bands, or when lifting anything heavy. Remember that your flexibility is not what it once was, so respect your years with caution.

**Respect rest:** You need a brief rest between each set of reps, to give your muscles a chance to reoxygenate, and enable you to do the next set effectively. Of even greater importance is the need for you to rest for at least a full day between resistance workouts involving each muscle group, to allow hypertrophy to repair, rebuild, and make you a little bit stronger. If you are injured make rest your priority, to get you back to your regular routine sooner.

**Include aerobics:** in your weekly routine to increase your resistance to diseases, and potentially keep you alive longer, and able to enjoy a higher quality of life. Try to get at least 75 minutes of vigorous cardiovascular training into your weekly schedule, or 150 minutes at a moderate pace.

**You are what you eat:** so eat well, and in moderation. Read up on the Mediterranean and DASH diets for knowledge and recipe ideas, and don't be seduced by the risky fad diets that keep emerging online and in bookstores.

## *Spread the Word*

If you enjoyed this book as much as I have enjoyed writing it, and if you feel (as I surely hope) that the resistance bands training you've received here will positively improve your lifestyle and your life, please tell others.

Spread the word by referrals to friends, family, and other seniors (and soon-to-be seniors) whom you know, and who you think can benefit.

## Our Community:

To be one of the first people to receive notification of future books in the series "For Seniors 50, 60 and Beyond" when they are released join our community. I'll personally notify you as soon the next book in the series is available. Our monthly newsletter also contains tip, tricks and advice to help you on your fitness journey.

As a member you have access to the exercise videos directly from our website ***www.iaa.pub*****,** without the need to scan individual QR codes within the book. Plus **Exclusive Members Access** to workout videos showing the exercises contained in each of the 32 workouts (not available from within the book), a great reference and time saver!

Finally, I wish to thank you so much for reading *Resistance Bands for Seniors 50, 60 and Beyond*. It was written to provide helpful information to seniors, and I hope that you'll use what you've learned in this book to build strength, improve balance as well as to look and feel years younger, boosting your confidence!

**I have a favor to ask:**

Would you please take a couple of minutes to write a review of this book on Amazon? I'll be checking the reviews personally and your honest feedback will help me better help others on their fitness journey.

## To leave a review:

You can either:

- Scan the QR Code on your mobile

- visit Amazon's website, search for *Resistance Bands for Seniors 50, 60 and Beyond*. Click the link for this book, scroll down, and click on "Write a Customer Review."

Thank you very much, and I look forward to reading your comments!

David O'Connor

## For Seniors 50, 60 and Beyond

BOOK SERIES

*Book 1:* **Fitness For Seniors 50, 60 and Beyond**

It's never too early to improve your fitness and definitely never to late to start. Consider this a fitness guide book, dip into to its sections as and when required.

*Book 2*: **Resistance Bands For Seniors 50, 60 and Beyond**

Strength and flexibility training without the need to purchase expensive weights and with less risk of injury, or a gym membership.

*Book 3*: **Balance Exercise For Seniors 50, 60 and Beyond**

Improve your balance to significantly reduce the risk and overcome the fear of falling. Live an active life in your golden years with increased self-confidence.

*Book 4*: **Chair Yoga For Seniors 50, 60 and Beyond**

All the benefits of yoga achievable while sitting or using a chair for additional support. Chair yoga offers variations that are perfect for seniors, even for those with limited mobility.

*Book 5*: **Stretching For Seniors 50, 60 and Beyond**

Stretches to improve flexibility, balance, mobility and reduce muscle pain for beginner through to advanced practitioners. Stretching helps release muscle tension, soreness and reduces the risk of injury.

*Book 6*: **Core Training For Seniors 50, 60 and Beyond**

A strong core stabilizes your entire body, providing better balance and posture. Core strength is essential at any age but especially as you get older and your risk of falling increases.

An overview of the For Seniors 50, 60 and Beyond book series is available at www.iaa.pub or scan the QR code.

**SCAN FOR BOOK INFORMATION**

# Glossary

**Advanced Training.** Resistance exercises for experienced individuals who have mastered the less complex and challenging groups of exercises; in addition to complexity, advanced training depends on higher levels of resistance.

**Aerobic Exercise.** Also called cardiovascular conditioning; aerobics are performed at a pace for a sustained period, with the objective of elevating the heart rate, and pumping more oxygen-rich blood through the heart to the muscles to help prevent heart disease, obesity, type 2 diabetes, and other diseases. Examples: Running, ellipticals cycling.

**Beginner Training.** A series of relatively simple and easy resistance exercises that are used to start a training program, and familiarize the user with usage of the various bands and tubes.

**Calisthenics.** A form of resistance exercises that use minimal or no equipment; relying instead on a person's body weight to provide the resistance force. Push ups, crunches, squats, and planks are examples.

**Cardiovascular Conditioning.** See Aerobic Exercise.

**Free Weights.** Dumbbells, barbells, and kettle weights used in the resistance training called weightlifting, and distinguished from weight cable machines generally found in gyms and fitness centers, which provide guided movements.

**Hypertrophy.** The intramuscular process of breaking down muscle cells and fibers as a result of resistance training, followed by rebuilding and overbuilding with added protein; it occurs during a rest of 48 hours following a hard resistance workout.

**Intermediate Resistance.** A series of resistance exercises that are more complex and challenging than beginner movements, and require a higher level of strength and a better sense of balance.

**Managed breathing.** Conscious inhalation with the abdomen and diaphragm extended outward to increase lung capacity, and exhalation with the abdomen and diaphragm tightly contracted to fully empty the lungs; used in yoga and other exercises.

**Mediterranean Diet.** A widely recommended dietary and lifestyle practice based on populations, whose health and longevity are above average; includes a wide range of unprocessed whole grains, vegetables and fruits, nuts and seeds, beans, fish, low fat dairy, eggs, and olive oil.

**Monounsaturated Fats.** A form of fat, generally an oil at room temperature, which is credited with lowering

LDL ("bad") cholesterol and raising HDL ("good") cholesterol, and therefore recommended for heart health. Abundant in extra virgin olive oil, canola oil and avocados.

**Polyunsaturated Fats.** Usually an oil at room temperature, also credited with lowering LDL (bad) cholesterol and raising HDL (good) cholesterol, and therefore recommended for heart health. Found in corn oil, sunflower oil, soybean oil, safflower oil, and peanut oil.

*Note:* Both mono and polyunsaturated oils are considered heart healthy; but recently monounsaturated oil has gained a reputation of being the more effective. New studies indicate that both types are equally beneficial, per *VeryWell Health* (2022).

**Reps and Sets.** 1 cycle of a resistance exercise is a repetition, or rep, such as raising and lowering a weight one time; a series of continued reps, such as 10 bicep curls or 12 push ups, is a set. A typical routine is three sets of 8 to 12 reps.

**Resistance Bands.** Stretchable flat and tubular lengths of a rubber or latex-based material that provide varying levels of resistance during exercise; some (tubes, primarily) have handles, and most bands are color-coded to designate resistance levels.

**Resistance Training.** These are exercises that use free weights, cable machines, or resistance bands and tubes to exhaust muscles to make them stronger, build endurance and make connective tendons, joints and ligaments more flexible and resilient.

**RICE Method.** A widely recommended procedure for treating injuries to muscles and joints: Rest, Ice, Compression, Elevation.

**Saturated Fats.** Typically solid at room temperature, and associated with elevated levels of LDL (bad) cholesterol and triglycerides, and resultant buildup of plaque in the coronary arteries: a serious form of heart disease. Found in meats and full fat dairy products, and in coconut and palm oils.

**Stretching.** A form of exercise that is distinguished from resistance and aerobic training; its objective is to lengthen and flex muscles, and connective tissues and joints to increase ranges of motion, and prevent injuries and improve performance. (See Yoga).

**VO2 Max.** The highest level your pulse can achieve under extreme stress; it is used to calculate your ideal heartbeat during aerobic exercise, which is generally 65% of 220 minus your age.

**Warmups.** Any exercise or stretching that is performed before resistance or aerobic training, to increase flexibility, and begin to oxygenate the heart and skeletal muscles.

**Yoga.** An ancient practice of stretches and poses (called *asanas*) originating in India and Asia, and very popular worldwide today. The focus is on managed breathing, concentration, balance, and flexibility. Yoga is a good supplement to resistance training.

# References

AZ Quotes. (2022). *Motivational inspirational sports quotes.*

https://www.azquotes.com/quotes/topics/motivational-inspirational-sports.html

Ali, M. (2011, February 3). *Top 25 quotes by Muhammad Ali (of 544)*. AZ Quotes.

https://www.azquotes.com/author/242-Muhammad_Ali

Bodybuilding.com (2021, January 20). *Bodybuilding.com's highest rated resistance band workouts.*

https://www.bodybuilding.com/content/best-resistance-band-workouts.html

BodyGym. (2022). *Before and after results of using resistance bands.*

https://moveyourself.bodygym.com/post/before-and-after-results-using-resistance-bands

Cleveland Clinic. (2022, May 4). *How effective are resistance bands for strength training?* Health Essentials from Cleveland Clinic.

https://health.clevelandclinic.org/should-you-try-resistance-bands-for-strength-training/

Article adapted from Cleveland Clinic Men's Health Advisor

Clifton. T. (2021, June 25). *Resistance band workouts for abs: 11 Exercises to try*. Healthline.

https://www.healthline.com/health/fitness/resistance-band-workouts-abs

Fetters, K. A. (2022, March 29). *The total-body resistance band workout*. Silver Sneakers.

https://www.silversneakers.com/blog/total-body-resistance-band-workout-older-adults/

Fetters, K. A. (2021, October 17). *7 Quick moves to do before every strength workout*. Silver Sneakers.

https://www.silversneakers.com/blog/7-quick-moves-to-do-before-every-strength-workout/

Lerner, A. (2018, April 24). *The beginner's guide to exercise bands*. Silver Sneakers.

https://www.silversneakers.com/blog/pick-right-resistance-band/

Lopes, J. S. S., Machado, A. F., Micheletti, J. K., de Almeida, A. C., Cavina, A. P., & Pastre, C. M. (2019, February 19). *Effects of training with elastic resistance versus conventional resistance on muscular strength: A systematic review and meta-analysis*. SAGE Open

Medicine, 7(PMC6383082), 205031211983111. National Institute of Health (NIH).

https://doi.org/10.1177/2050312119831116

Lyon, R. A. (2022, August 18). *Do resistance bands build bone density?* Senior Fitness.

https://www.seniorfitness.org/do-resistance-bands-build-bone-density/

Machowsky, J. (2022, March 29). *The total-body resistance band workout*. Silver Sneakers.

https://www.silversneakers.com/blog/total-body-resistance-band-workout-older-adults/

Migala, J. (2022, April 13). *How to get started with resistance band workouts: An absolute beginner's guide*. Everyday Health.

https://www.everydayhealth.com/fitness/how-to-get-started-with-resistance-band-workouts-an-absolute-beginners-guide/

Moghe, S. (2022, August 28). *DASH diet vs. Mediterranean diet*. Health Plugged.

https://healthplugged.com/dash-diet-mediterranean-diet/

Moll, J. (2022, August 24). *Saturated vs. unsaturated fats*. VeryWell Health.

https://www.verywellhealth.com/difference-between-saturated-fats-and-unsaturated-fats-697517

Porter, E. (2020, September 8). *9 Types of resistance bands and when to use each of them*. Trusty Spotter.

https://trustyspotter.com/blog/types-of-resistance-bands/

Samuel, E., et al. (2022, August 17). *56 Resistance bands moves you can do at home*. Men's Health.

https://www.menshealth.com/fitness/a32093962/resistance-band-workouts/

Samuels, M. (2013, October 19). *Exercises for ancillary muscles*. SportsRec.

https://www.sportsrec.com/exercises-ancillary-muscles-12320280.html

Stephens, D'A. (2022, March 12). *This 20-minute resistance band workout actually feels harder than weights*. Livestrong.

https://www.livestrong.com/article/13770019-20-minute-advanced-resistance-band-workout/

Stivey, G. (2022, April 20). *How to use resistance bands for injury recovery*. GND Fitness.

https://gndfit.com/blogs/gnd-fitness/how-to-use-resistance-bands-for-injury-recovery?shpxid=ab450fa2-f3d3-4df5-bfec-90020a13bf08

TB12 Team. (2021, February 10). *Tom Brady workout: His 9-exercise high-intensity favorite.*

https://tb12sports.com/blogs/tb12/tom-brady-workout

Waehner, J. (2022, June 22). *Beginner's total body resistance band workout*. Very Well Fit.

https://www.verywellfit.com/beginner-total-body-resistance-band-workout-1231110

WebMD. (2022). *Best resistance band exercises for beginners.*

https://www.webmd.com/fitness-exercise/resistance-bands-exercises-beginners#1

WebMD. (2021, April 24). *What is the RICE method for injuries?*

https://www.webmd.com/first-aid/rice-method-injuries

Yes2Next. (2022, August 4). *10 Chair resistance band exercises.*

https://yes2next.com/fitness-joy/resistance-bands

Printed in Great Britain
by Amazon

29413277R00145